THREE MEN
on an
ISLAND

THREE MEN
on an
ISLAND

•

WRITTEN AND ILLUSTRATED
BY
JAMES MACINTYRE

To Ed.
Thanks for your generosity
in New York

James MacIntyre

THE
BLACKSTAFF
PRESS

BELFAST

First published in October 1996 by
The Blackstaff Press Limited
3 Galway Park, Dundonald, Belfast BT16 0AN, Northern Ireland
with the assistance of
The Arts Council of Northern Ireland
Reprinted November 1996

Typeset by Techniset Typesetters, Newton-le-Willows, Merseyside

Printed in Northern Ireland by W. & G. Baird Limited

A CIP catalogue record for this book
is available from the British Library

ISBN 0-85640-582-5

for Mike,
Seán and Andrew

PREFACE

This is the story of three artists on an island called Inishlacken off Roundstone in Connemara during the summer of 1951 – Gerard Dillon, George Campbell and myself, James MacIntyre. We were on the island because Gerard had been given the use of a cottage for twelve months as part payment for a painting. In the years immediately after the Second World War the cost of living, compared with that of today, was ludicrously low. Even so, the remuneration needed to survive in a life style that was notoriously fragile was very difficult to achieve. George and Gerard were ten years older than me and had started to make their mark in the art world. They were still on the treadmill but their early hardships were behind them and they were achieving a certain amount of success in Belfast and Dublin. It had been a hard grind, surviving, making a name in the postwar years. As for myself, I was still trying to keep a foothold on the bottom rungs of the ladder, encouraged to keep going by a few favourable reviews. We all struggled through the early years of making a career out of painting pictures.

There were misfortunes galore as we battled against the barriers that kept us unknown to the acclaim that we thought we merited but, together, we were a merry crowd. Lots of laughter broke the gloom, arguments of Byzantine complexity, tolerance of each other's shortcomings and excesses and the myriad aspects of friendship and creativity. All part of a group sharing a common zeal.

But we lived through those early days that made and shaped us and I hope this book shows some of the enjoyment we got from a tiny portion of them.

1

I was young, skint and spearing a breakfast sausage and tatie bread as the
letters clattered through our brass letter box, skittering across the linoleum
onto the old bristle mat. The important one, the one addressed to me in
bold handwriting, bore a Southern Irish stamp stuck on askew. The office of
origin was smudged but the date was clear enough – 16 April 1951 – and I
recognised Gerard Dillon's script. His Christmas card had come from Dublin
but this letter was headed Inishlacken island, Roundstone, Connemara. Just
one page – unusual for Gerard, as he normally rambled over four, decorating
them with little drawings.

Dear Jim
Would you like a bed for a month or six weeks on Inishlacken? It's a mile
off Roundstone in the Atlantic. You'll love it. Stone walls, thatched
cottages, a real peasant life, just up your street. You'll need about £15 for
expenses, there's no rent as I have it for the year. Try to get over next
month. Drop me a line when you are coming.
   Yours
   Gerard

P.S. I need some colours, Flake White, Yellow Ochre, Burnt Umber.
Bring them with you.

Bloody pigs might fly, I thought. In my state of financial insecurity, I had as
much chance of going to the moon, but it was difficult not to daydream.

Islands had always fascinated me. Inishlacken would be like the pictures of the Blasket Islands in a book I had borrowed from the local library the previous week. I found an atlas in a cupboard. Where was Roundstone? On the west coast of Ireland about forty miles north-west of Galway. There were a few little dots off the coast too small to be named. With Belfast on the north-east coast and Roundstone in the middle of the west coast, there was no way I could get there in one day. Railway to Dublin, then across to Galway. End of the line. The tortuous road west would be by a country bus so I would have to spend a night in either Dublin or Galway. A nice dream, I thought, but there was no chance of me raising the money to get to Roundstone. My studio was crammed with unsold paintings; buyers for a young artist's work were as scarce as snowballs in hell.

A fortnight later I went to the John Magee Gallery in Donegall Square West in Belfast to see if they had sold the two paintings they had accepted just before Christmas. Old John was as tight as a Lambeg drum and although he had sold a few pictures before, I thought these two might be difficult to move. I intended taking them back and replacing them with two of my latest ones.

'No, I don't think they have been sold, but I'll check,' said an apologetic assistant.

So much for my dreams. Glumly, I watched her head for the storeroom. For twenty-five minutes I sat, sunk into a plush settee in the upper gallery, and watched her agitated progress from the gallery to the store, office to shop, shop to office, without a glance in my direction. Something was amiss. Suddenly a

grim-faced John Magee strode up to me with a fistful of notes. He thrust them at me with no sign of enthusiasm.

'Here, sign for your seventeen pounds.'

He was unaware that losing my paintings had given me a summer with Gerard on Inishlacken. Minutes later, a helpful assistant at the Irish Tourist Board office spread a map, charting my trip into the unknown west. My pocket would be twelve and sixpence lighter for a return trip from Belfast to Dublin; from Dublin to Roundstone by train and bus, one pound. Limited connections meant an overnight stay in Dublin.

A few days later, as I was leaving the gallery at 55A Donegall Place, I saw the ample figure of old W.R. Gordon. He was a retired art teacher who worked in the gallery occasionally as custodian. I mounted the stairway two at a time, unable to contain myself with the good news. He was always interested in young artists. His bushy eyebrows wiggling, a large smile bending his face, he listened as I related Magee's misfortune.

'Bulmer Hobson lives in Roundstone,' he confided. 'I haven't seen him in years. Would you look him up, give him my best regards and find out how he is.'

'Is he an artist?'

'No, but he writes – among other things.'

'Like what?'

W.R. passed a slow grin. 'Tell you what, ask him yourself.'

I made my plans. Sunday morning tramcars in 1951 did not commence their first run until 8.30 a.m., too late for me to catch the nine o'clock train to Dublin. A three-mile walk with a loaded rucksack would stretch my legs. I prayed fervently for a dry morning. I loathed rain of any kind, soft or heavy. Departure day, eagerly awaited, dawned bright, with Divis Mountain shimmering in the haze.

'Watch yourself and don't go doing anything daft on that island.' My ma leaned on the gate post, casting a critical eye over me. 'You might have cleaned those boots a bit better – and that raincoat will be a mass of wrinkles tied up like that. God only knows what the people on that island will think of you.'

My eyeballs rolled. I had heard it all before.

'I'll send you a card when I get there but don't expect to see me for a month or so.'

The main road sloped downhill towards the city. Endless streets of closed doors and drawn blinds, with not a sinner in sight, echoed to the clatter of my steel-shod boots. Shankill graveyard could muster more life than a Belfast Sunday morning, I thought to myself. The Great Northern Railway station, its giant pillars straddling wide stone steps, showed little sign of life, either. Red-faced with exertion, a couple of people humped heavy suitcases up the final steps to the platform. Inside, passengers sat around with heaps of brown paper parcels and bulging suitcases, waiting patiently for the ticket collector to open the ornate gates and hang up the destination board. A mizzle of hissing steam, whistles and clanking buffers finally announced that a corridor train had threaded its way up the platform and shuddered to a halt. I dumped my

rucksack in the corded rack and sank blissfully into a corner seat. Sepia views of Killarney and the Mourne Mountains stared back at me above the plush buttoned upholstery.

Two hours later, a hard-faced, unsmiling customs officer came into the coach at the border. 'Anything to declare?' he demanded.

I shook my head but he paused, a questioning eyebrow raised as he saw my rucksack.

'What's in that?' he asked suspiciously.

'I'm going on a trip to the west of Ireland for a month. It's my clothes and things.'

His peaked cap, cocked over one eye, slid back as he reached up and chalked a yellow line across the rucksack. Obviously, one look was enough to convince him that searching me for contraband was a waste of time and effort.

In Dublin, although it was Sunday, hordes of people were wandering up and down O'Connell Street. The cyclists amazed me. They rolled along in droves, seemingly oblivious to dashing pedestrians and the odd car that became trapped amongst them. George and Madge Campbell had offered me a bed for the night, but since it was my first visit to Dublin, I made a few wrong turns before I found their flat. We had something to celebrate. George had just had a successful exhibition in the Victor Waddington Galleries

Madge and George Campbell, 1951

in Dublin. Over pints of Guinness we toasted his good fortune, while Madge laid plates of sausages, eggs and spuds before us. We cracked about people, places and bits of news until George suddenly announced that he was coming to Roundstone with me. I was delighted. We would have a hell of a time. I couldn't wait to get there.

Next morning we were on the nine o'clock train to Galway. It arrived at one o'clock and the bus for Roundstone did not leave until two o'clock, so there was time to walk around the town and have a sandwich and a pint. I was determined not to miss anything on this trip so we got the front seats on the old prewar Dennis. Country folk, heavily laden with packages, struggled aboard, while their overflow baggage was hoisted onto the roof rack. Gears crunched into an obstinate mesh, jolting us forward in our seats, the engine shuddered as it slowly gathered speed, rolling us toward the open countryside.

With Roundstone over fifty miles away, and at the rate we were travelling, I reckoned it would be midnight before we got there. Every crossroads was a stopping point. People clambered on and off, the conductor unloading their luggage to the accompaniment of a torrent of good-natured comment. Everyone seemed to know everyone else, making the bus a kind of travelling club. As we journeyed further and further westward, I began to notice that the stone-walled fields were getting smaller; boulders poked up through the scanty grass, and in the background mountains rimmed the horizon.

Laboriously, the old bus topped a steep hill, lurched over the crest, and suddenly the windscreen was filled with a wide arc of ocean. Right across the horizon the Atlantic glittered in the sun. At last, I thought, after three hours on the road, we must be nearing Roundstone. We were not, but the view made up for the sores on my bum and the cramp in my knees. Whins splashed patches of yellow over stone walls shot with crimson fuchsia; whitewashed cottages capped with thatch were scattered higgledy-piggledy, their gable ends propped up by mounds of brown turf. Everywhere there were stones – millions of them, of all shapes and sizes, tumbling down the hillsides, embedded deep in the ground and lit by shafts of sunlight lancing through gaps in the stone walls. There were humps and hollows, high hillocks, odd, straggly bushes flattened into a permanent stoop by the westerly wind. Around it all, like a frame, was a blue background of mountains shimmering in the afternoon sun. Now I knew where all the Paul Henry blues and greys had come from. I could see his pictures painting themselves before my eyes.

Roundstone harbour

I clutched George's arm. 'Would you look at that' – painting after painting shot past me like shooting stars, seen for a fraction of a second, to be replaced by another, and then another. I had never, in all my life, encountered a landscape like this. The Mournes had a slumbering grandeur, but this wilderness, the desolation, the raw colour and stark composition had me punch drunk.

My watch said that we should have arrived in Roundstone but none of the multitudinous signposts mentioned the town's name. We were getting nearer to the coast. The bus ambled round a tight corner and stopped suddenly for the hundredth flock of sheep. A sea of black, bobbing heads herded by a man on an old bicycle swept round us, thumping their way past the bus. A leaning telegraph pole carried a road sign which announced that Roundstone was five miles away. Irish miles. The highway was barely wide enough to let oncoming traffic pass. Luckily, there was none, as we twisted and turned, hugging the rugged coastline. Tall trees camouflaged a sharp bend, slowing the bus to a crawl as we entered a dome of interwoven branches and leaves. Beyond the thick foliage, behind wrought-iron gates, the white gables of a large house reflected the evening sun. George commented that it was a perfect setting for an artist's house.

We had arrived. Back in the sunlight the road curved in front of us to a huddle of houses leapfrogging up a steep hill overlooking a granite-walled harbour berthing a collection of gaily coloured fishing boats. It was fine weather but the swaying masts and booms reminded us of the Atlantic swell between us and our island destination.

At last the engine growled, spat and died after a final shudder and we stopped outside a pub festooned with advertising. After four hours of sweltering, swaying travel my legs felt permanently bent and I was as stiff as a poker.

'What kept you?' Gerard was behind us, duncher cocked at a rakish angle, his face the colour of a chestnut, and a wide grin under his moustache. He was wearing a cream Aran sweater pulled low over his backside, heavy woollen trousers and a pair of boots a navvy would have been proud to own.

We explained the tortuously slow progress of the bus.

Gerard nodded towards a broad-shouldered man leaning against the pub door. 'Meet Michael Woods. He lives on the island. I've got him to help me row the currach.'

Shaking hands with Michael was like putting your hand in a vice. Testing his strength daily against the Atlantic had given him shoulders and neck muscles

like a bull. He seemed a bit shy with these two foreigners who had been
suddenly thrust upon him.

'We'll have a pint to set us up for the journey,' Gerard said, leading the way
to the bar.

Two hours and three pints of Guinness later we headed for the harbour. My
head was spinning. The bar had run out of sandwiches and my belly thought
my throat had been cut. After seven hours without solid food I was starving.

A flight of stone steps led down the harbour wall to our currach moored at
the end of a long rope. Michael hauled it alongside the steps, holding it close
to the wall as we put our luggage aboard. The hairs on the back of my neck
stood up in fright when I looked at the light wooden framework supporting
a tarred canvas hull that was going to transport the four of us across the Atlantic
to Inishlacken. I was not reassured when Gerard warned us to keep our feet
on the centre slats. I could imagine my steel toecaps poking a hole in the
canvas and so plunging us to a watery grave. I was even more alarmed when I
noticed how far the currach settled in the water when the four of us got
aboard with Michael in the bow, Gerard next to him, and George and me in
the stern. It did not seem to worry Michael, and with a mighty thrust, he sent
us skimming out into the harbour.

George seemed to be even more nervous than me. He sat rigid, as if his life
depended on not uttering a word, clutching his guitar case as though, should
the worst befall, it might bear him safely back to the shore. The Atlantic was
kind to us. With Michael and Gerard on the oars, rowing cross-handed in the

island style, we headed for the open sea over a gentle swell, leaving a trail of bubbles in our wake.

It was a beautiful evening, without a breath of wind. A cloud of seagulls dipped and curtsied to see us on our way. I began to feel more at ease. This, I reasoned, was an everyday occurrence for the islanders, summer and winter. I resolutely shut out of my mind the thought of what it might be like in half a gale. Gerard rested on his oars, taking a breather, although Michael carried on pulling us across the water like a well-oiled machine. Familiarity, strength and constant practice made it look easy.

'This is the long way round,' Gerard said. 'There's a shorter way straight from the island to a wee beach outside Roundstone but we thought it would be easier to pick up you and your luggage from the harbour.' He hunched his back, picking up the stroke again.

Inishlacken sat on the ocean, a long grey sliver of rock patched with green, rising in humps up to the centre. There were no trees. Outlined against a pale blue sky, the empty window frames of a gaunt, roofless ruin stared out to sea. Hard by was a ribbon of pearly sand a few hundred yards long and massive rocks sheltering the gable ends of thatched cottages. They huddled together about the boulder-littered shoreline. Wisps of turf smoke drifted straight up into the still, evening air.

About three hundred yards off the island I could see Michael glancing over his shoulder and lining up the currach with the big ruin. Squinting into the evening sun, I tried to see what he was looking for among the fissured rocks and seaweed-covered boulders. Waves splashed against a concrete harbour wall but I could see no entrance until we got closer when a gap, barely ten feet wide, opened up, leading to a horseshoe-shaped harbour. Michael's expertise took us safely through into tranquil water. The gently sloping beach was rimmed with grass around its curved perimeter. Half a dozen black currachs sprawled upside down, their bows buried in white dog daisies. Stone walls lined the concrete slipway going up the grass-covered bank. Sitting on top of the bank was a white-painted cottage with a slate roof, a bright blue door

and window frames to match. I sat in the currach, arms on my knees, soaking in the scene, as Michael leapt out to haul us up onto the soft sand. His passengers, lacking the grace that comes with practice, sprangled in confusion behind him. Once the flimsy craft was unloaded, it was tipped upside down with the others. We sank down on the grass for a smoke before bidding farewell to Michael.

The path to the cottage wound between half-buried rocks, their round sides speckled with green and brown lichen. A weathered latch gate in a stone wall led into a garden full of wild flowers. It faced the open sea, the high harbour wall etching a sharp line against the smudged purple of the Twelve Bens on the horizon. The plastered white walls were tinged by the setting sun. There was no curtain at the window but two stone jars sat there, crammed with more wild flowers. Their heads were entangled in a cord net holding a green fishing buoy suspended from the window frame. There was no knocker on the door, no lock or letter box, only an enormous curved black latch. This was Inishlacken, island of the lakes.

A massive fireplace dominated the living room of our cottage. The turf fire it housed, a lazy spiral of blue smoke climbing the stack and scenting the entire cottage, was the centre of our existence, our only source of heat and means of cooking. From the gloomy depths of the chimney breast a chain, suspended from a crossbar, carried a heavy black kettle. On either side of the fireplace were the doors that led to the two bedrooms. The living room had one substantial piece of furniture, the dresser, which took up most of the back wall facing the fireplace. Three shelves held plates, saucers and egg cups. Five mugs dangled from hooks and a dozen upturned glasses stood on the bottom shelf.

The basin stood on a wide work top covered with patterned oilcloth. At the far end was a breadboard and half a loaf. The bottom half of the dresser had two wooden doors held shut by swivels. Inside, one shelf held a big enamel jug for buttermilk and a box for the cutlery. The lower shelf held spuds, carrots and onions, tins of soup, beans, peas, corned beef and other odds and ends. In the centre of the room was a sturdy wooden table. Dents and scratches had etched the surface, the original square edges long since rounded with constant use. On the flagged floor sat a few chairs and in the corner, Gerard's bed, which doubled as a settee, was the only concession to comfort.

Gerard suggested a cup of tea and a bap and unhooked the kettle, moving it a few links down the chain until its flat bottom rested on the fire. He gave the fire a stir with the poker. 'See this fire, it's never to be allowed to go out because it's hell to light again. It's only been out once since I got here. And another thing' – he pointed to the sash window opposite the door – 'you don't open that window and the door at the same time. If you do, the draught blows the turf dust everywhere. It sticks to oils and makes a hell of a mess.'

We talked over mugs of tea and baps wedged with hunks of cheese, giving Gerard the latest art news and scandal from Belfast and Dublin. He had been on Inishlacken since February, with only letters from his numerous friends for contact, so he relished all the titbits we provided.

The food and drink and the fire were unwinding George and myself, but Gerard suddenly jumped up from the bed: 'Come on, I'll show you the island before it gets dark.'

I was happy to sit smoking my pipe but he seemed so keen, even excited, at the prospect of giving us a conducted tour of the 'last parish before New York' that we had to go.

The sun had vanished, leaving streaks of orange and crimson trailing across the sky. Somewhere a sheep bleated and a donkey hee-hawed in answer. A path lined by stone walls led from the gate up to a slight rise past the harbour wall towards a thatched cottage perched on a hillock. Here the path widened enough to take a donkey and cart. This, Gerard explained, was the road that hugged the shore around the island. It was just over a mile long. Dew speckled the scant grass verges of the road and black cows, settled down for the night, watched us, twitching ears scattering midges as we clattered by. From the high

ground we could see most of the island spread around us. All the cottages were close to the sea, some huddled together, others so far apart that they were barely visible in the purple shadows cast by the walls and the massive boulders. Oil lamps glittered through uncurtained windows, like miniature lanterns in the growing darkness. The light was fading fast, shuttling eerie shadows over hillocks, broken walls and boulders shaping this lunar landscape. We stumbled along in the semi-darkness, relieved that our tour of the island was over. Stars studded a velvet sky and a low moon gave our cottage a ghostly sheen.

Once inside, we lit the oil lamps and heaped the fire with turf to last all night. In its warmth the other two sat yarning but I lit a candle and dragged my weary bones to bed. As I lay recalling the day's happenings, I was slowly aware of a dull pounding noise, as regular as a metronome, thumping close by. It took me a while to work out what the sound was: it was the Atlantic breakers crashing on the beach less than fifty yards from my head. A very different world from the one at home. There, the main road outside echoed to the clangs and rattles of trams speeding downhill at all hours of the night and morning, making a racket that would waken the dead. But it was a familiar barrage. Here, without my accustomed serenade, I could not get to sleep. Through a slit in the curtain a yellow moon hung between the bars of the window frame. The bedsprings twanged deep in the hard mattress as I rolled onto one side, one ear buried in the pillow, the other smothered by the blanket tugged over my head. The waves did send me to sleep in the end, the rhythmic throbbing dying away as I slid into a dreamless void.

When I awoke next morning, a shaft of sunlight slanted down the wall and angled across the flagged floor. There was not a sound – apart from the snores and snorts of George in the adjoining bedroom. Slipping out of bed, I parted the curtains, and nearly jumped out of my skin at the sight of a big white and ginger cat staring back at me. This, I learnt later, was Suzy Blue Hole, discerningly named because of the colour of part of her anatomy. I went into the main room, and vigorous squeezing of a large pair of bellows soon roused a flame in the hearth. With more turf piled on, I lowered the kettle. I would have a boiled egg and toast for breakfast. Gerard looked out for the count, so I tiptoed round, trying not to wake him, but he suddenly propped himself up on one elbow.

'It's time I was up,' he replied to my apologies. 'Will you go easy with that bucket of water. It's all we've got.'

'Don't worry. Tell me where to go and I'll get it filled.'

'You can't,' he responded.

I considered this surprising statement for a few seconds before asking why I could not fetch a bucket of water.

'Because we get it from the beach and the tide is in. We can't get fresh water until it goes out.'

I must have had a blank look on my face as I tried to figure out how we could get fresh water from a beach swept by the Atlantic. Gerard explained that there was an underground stream that fed a well at the top of the beach. It was contained by a ring of boulders, which the tide unfortunately covered at its highest, but when it went out the fresh water bubbled up. I shook my head in amazement at this seeming reversal of the natural order of things.

'You'll soon know the tides better than the clock. Put another egg on for me. I'll give the porridge a rest this morning.'

The toast turned a golden brown. Spread liberally with yellow butter and cheese, my taste buds started to drool at the sight as I cracked open my egg.

'In the name of Jesus,' I shrieked, 'will you look at this egg!'

The yolk was like a huge bloodshot eye with angry red streaks radiating outwards into the pale white. I probed gingerly with my spoon at the surface of the yolk and found that it was a soft gory mess underneath.

'That's enough to give you the jandies just looking at it! I'm not eating that mess.'

'That's what happens when a hen has a heart attack,' Gerard observed.

I studied my egg in silence while I grappled with his medical diagnosis. Then he cracked open the top of his own egg. Another bloodshot eye stared back at us – a dead ringer for mine. The look on my face made Gerard erupt into a roar of laughter. He dug into his egg, oblivious of its bloody hue. Between mouthfuls of toast he explained the phenomenon. It seemed that the hens lived on a diet of seaweed and mulch, which had a high iodine content, and that was what produced the crimson yolk. Once you got used to it, he assured me, you never gave it a second thought.

Outside, it was a glorious morning; nothing stirred, and an unbelievable silence hung in the air as we creaked onto the long garden bench. A butterfly sunned itself on the wall, hover flies darted here and there. Suzy Blue Hole, curled in a ball, slept half-hidden by the wild yellow irises clustered around the wall. Beyond the harbour wall, on the rim of a sparkling Atlantic, the horizon shone like a silver ring. A grey smudge crawled across it, heading for some unknown fishing ground. We sprawled in the sun, eyes closed as we soaked up its warmth, almost dropping off to sleep again.

I roused myself. 'We've got a funny water supply, funny eggs. Is there anything else that's funny we should know about?'

Gerard gave me a sideways look. 'Aah . . . there is.'

'What?'

'There's no loo.'

'You're kidding!'

'No, there's no bog. I don't think there's one on the whole island. Not the sort you are used to.'

'I thought that lean-to round the back was the bog house.'

'That's the coal house. It's so full of turf that the door won't close.'

'No po under the bed?'

'No, but there's plenty of big rocks and walls about. Just get down behind one of those.'

George had woken up and came to join us. 'Suppose the sky is pissing rain on you?' he asked.

'Just hunker further down on the side away from the wind. It's a lovely feeling having your bum tickled by wet grass.'

I laughed. I was reminded of summer camps in the Boy Scouts; digging holes in the ground and surrounding them with a sacking screen. However, Gerard enlightened me, Inishlacken was different. You would be lucky to dig a hole nine inches deep before the thin soil gave way to solid rock.

'Spread it around in wee pyramids,' Gerard advised.

George did not look too happy about these toilet arrangements but the talk about bogs had got him in a state where he had to start experimenting.

'One other thing,' Gerard added. 'Cover it up with loose stones. We don't want the whole island speckled with flying bumph.'

I looked at my watch. Eleven o'clock and I had not lifted a pencil. I had come here to work, not to sit soaking up the sun. I stared around. Where to begin? There were so many things to draw that I couldn't make up my mind in which direction to go. The answer to that problem seemed to be – anywhere.

'I'm getting my stuff and heading for those derelict cottages at the far end of the beach. I'll see what I can do with the watercolours.'

'Hold on a minute, Big Lad,' Gerard said.

When he called me that, it usually meant that I was going to get advice, whether I wanted it or not.

'Don't you go buck-leaping over those walls, because if you break a leg you could be in agony for a long time, and if you smash your skull, you could kick the bucket. The nearest hospital is fifteen miles away in Clifden. It's a slow run once you're on the road and we'd have to get you that far first. There's nothing like the Royal at the end of the road here, you know.'

He was beginning to sound just like my ma, I thought. However, it was good advice.

'Don't be too long. We're going across to Roundstone later for supplies,' he called after me.

Later, the smell of frying bacon floating in the air became too much for me and when I returned Gerard had produced a meal of spuds, bacon and sausages.

'How did you get on?' enquired George.

'Terrible,' I moaned. 'I don't know where to begin. There's so much material out there.'

Gerard grinned. 'Good – now we'll start learning something.'

I shook my head but he was right; over the ensuing weeks I learnt much.

Our dinner had barely settled when Gerard suddenly announced with a yell from inside the cottage that it was time we got off our backsides and learnt to do a bit of rowing. George, taking his ease on the bench, opened one eye and looked anything but enthusiastic.

Black-headed sheep stared and bolted through the nearest hole in a wall as we trooped down to the harbour. At the schoolhouse we stopped and I pointed to a slate plaque inscribed 1908. Silently, hands in pockets, eyes screwed tight against the glare of the sun, we gazed at the moss-ridden stone shell.

'Not much left of that,' I said. 'Surely some of the roof timbers and slates ought to be lying around.'

George ambled over for a closer look, disappearing inside. He emerged after a few minutes shrugging his shoulders. 'Damn all in there but grass. I reckon the islanders must have picked it clean once time and storms had reduced it to a wreck.'

Gerard pulled his duncher even further down over his eyes and said that we would ask Michael when it closed and how many pupils it had in its heyday. It was likely that he had been taught there himself. We could imagine a lone schoolmaster striding between the desks, a turf fire smouldering in the grate, chalk squeaking over slate, the pupils chanting their tables, the mischievous getting the cane and the joy as the bell signalled the end of another day's lessons. The children were now probably scattered to the next parish and far beyond the nearest embarkation post; the schoolmaster, perhaps, resting in Gorteen graveyard on the headland, keeping a kindly eye on his former domain.

'I think our cottage must have been the schoolmaster's house. Those walls must hold a few secrets. Have you seen any ghosts, Gerard?' I asked.

For a fleeting moment a strange looked passed over Gerard's eyes and he turned away.

'Have you?' I persisted.

'Naw, don't believe in them.'

'Just as well. If there's a banshee around here we've nowhere to run,' said George.

'Will you two come on and stop blethering about that school. We're going rowing, remember.' With that Gerard strode off toward the harbour, his head bent, staring at the ground.

'Hell roast it,' I muttered, 'he's upset. I should have kept my mouth shut.'

It was my turn to feel uneasy as I imagined being alone on the island through the long, dark winter nights, watching the flickering shadows cast by the dim oil lamps and the dancing flames from the turf fire whipped up by a howling gale thundering over the slates; the boom of the pounding surf on the beach; ominous noises coming down the chimney stack while the windows rattled in their frames. No wonder talk of banshees upset him.

Circling seagulls, Persil-white against the deep blue sky, screeched at the intrusion, as our thumping feet set harebells nodding by the path. A puttering engine announced the passing of a little red and white fishing boat, the fisherman giving us a friendly wave from the wheelhouse as it stuttered towards the horizon. Suzy Blue Hole scampered behind us at a safe distance, still uncertain about these strangers. Gerard unhitched the tow rope and tugged a wooden dinghy (which came with the cottage as well as the currach) to the granite steps of the harbour wall. He got in, holding it steady, while George and I gingerly stepped aboard. George took the bow thwart, I had the middle one, with Gerard in the stern to act as pilot and instructor. We shoved off, got the oars in the rowlocks, and started to put our backs into the transport business. The dinghy wheeled round in a circle.

'You're supposed to be heading out to sea, not up the bloody beach,' yelled Gerard. 'Relax, we've got a long way to row and we'll only do it by keeping together. Get your oars in the water together, take them out together. You can't stick them in and out when you feel like it. George, watch the Big Lad, take your time from him. You've got to row as a team.'

He shook his head in despair as George and I bumped and clattered, locking our oars together or else missing the water completely, the oars skittering water everywhere. However, we eventually got into some sort of rhythm, only to find ourselves heading straight for the rocks. We hadn't noticed that the harbour had a sharp bend before reaching the open sea. We were rowing in a straight line and now we had to turn.

L to R: George, Gerard and Suzy Blue Hole

'Jesus, you bloody eejits, you're going to wreck the boat!' Gerard's patience was beginning to fray. He said he hoped we would get to Roundstone tomorrow if we didn't make it today.

The lesson began again. Eventually, amid threats, strong language and reminders about our need for fresh supplies, we edged out into the open sea. By then Gerard was as exhausted as George and me. A few hundred yards offshore we had managed a rough sort of rhythm, with our oars dipping in together. George started to complain that the floor slats were too far apart for his boots to get a grip. He kept peering into the green abyss and asking how deep we thought it was. Progress was slow. Gerard thought that our present rate would get us into Roundstone by midnight and advised making for the nearest beach and walking from there. He pointed to a small beach on the headland, guarding the estuary.

Three-quarters of the way across, George suddenly hauled in his oars. 'My hands,' he groaned, 'look at the state of them already. They're starting to blister.'

We could see that they were red but there was no sign of a blister.

'If they get any worse,' he lamented, 'I'll not be able to play my guitar.'

'You know what's wrong with you?' Gerard grinned. 'It's your soft life; Madge has bloody spoilt you. Those lily-white paws haven't done a day's work since God knows when – if ever.'

George was indignant. 'What do you expect?' he yelled. 'I'm an artist, not a bloody road digger.'

'Come off it, you're a lazy bugger. Hard work would kill you. You just want an excuse to sit on your arse like a lord, with two silly buggers to ferry you hither and thither.' Gerard was smiling, obviously enjoying taking the mickey out of George. 'All right, if we spare your tender paws, you'll have to play your guitar when we want you to. Otherwise you start rowing again.'

Telling George was one thing, getting him to do it was another. We knew he would play his guitar only when he was in the mood. Gerard then offered to take George's place, but he refused to budge, saying that scrambling from stern to bow would upset the dinghy. It was at this point that I made my big mistake and offered to row the rest of the way myself. By the time we reached the little bay my oarsmanship had convinced the pair of them that I was a natural sailor, overflowing with energy. From then on I was the permanent ferryman.

We hauled the dinghy up beyond the high-water mark onto a grassy bank and set off for the village. With my rucksack slung over my back to take our shopping, we clambered through a forest of bracken onto a rough track with just enough room for us in single file. Ahead we could see the roofs of Roundstone. Dandelions were massed under the stone walls on the verges, the spindly stalks of an old hollyhock running wild strained upwards to the light and patches of lime-green foliage brightened the grey stone. Round a bend there was an old man poking among the first shoots of the potatoes sprouting from his lazy beds. He leaned on his spade and wished us the time of day through a cloud of smoke from his pipe as we ambled onto the main road.

Gerard pointed out a small bungalow surrounded by bushes and a hedge. 'I've made some friends there and have done drawings of the inside as well as outside. I can see a chance of a painting there.'

We followed his gaze but there was no sign of life at the curtained windows.

A painting did materialise later, however, to be called *The Yellow Bungalow*, and was purchased by the Ulster Museum. 'It paid the rent of my flat for four months,' he said of it.

In the village the main street sloped down to the harbour where the brightly coloured fishing boats were moored two abreast along the wall. Houses lined one side of the road as it curved away out of the village. To seaward, a myriad sparklets danced across the bay as a heat haze merged sea and sky in a hidden horizon. Beyond, the roller-coaster tips of the Twelve Bens were barely visible. As we crossed the road to the shops we could feel the tar sticking to our boots.

Gerard, the quartermaster, had a word of warning: 'Listen to me. This is a close-knit community and everybody knows what you're doing before you do it. So don't do all the shopping in one place – spread it around. Everybody gets to know you and it keeps them all happy.' He delivered his lecture standing in the middle of the pavement, nodding to folk as they passed. Suddenly, his head whipped round as he stared down the street. 'Jesus, it's the Father. I'll see you in Connolly's,' he said over his shoulder as he disappeared into an adjacent grocer's.

The shopping was a leisurely affair, frequently interrupted by queries about where we hailed from, what it was like in Belfast with all those people about, did we enjoy life on the island, the landscape, the weather, how long we

The Yellow Bungalow
by Gerard Dillon

were staying and were we not worried about being marooned? Some of the questions made us wonder what chance we had of seeing civilisation again. Three mad eejits of artists living on Inishlacken. The whole town knew everything about us within a day or so of our arrival.

Soon my rucksack felt like it weighed a ton and George was complaining about the shopping bag breaking his arm.

'There must be enough here to last us a month,' he declared as we headed for a big pint of Guinness in Connolly's bar.

It was pleasantly cool in the pub as, our hands wrapped round pint glasses, we watched Gerard deep in conversation with the barmaid, Carmel. He leaned back on his high stool as she burst out laughing. She looked across at us, then back to Gerard, who had a wide grin on his face. We wondered what the discourse was all about. He brought two more pints to the table and told us he had been telling her about our prowess as oarsmen. No wonder she was laughing. Gerard was good at embroidering a story.

George wanted to know why he had disappeared like a scalded cat earlier on.

'It's the priest. He's been after me for months to go to mass. I get a lecture every time we meet and I'm running out of excuses,' he lamented.

'Why can't you tell him you don't want to go?' George asked.

Gerard gazed sadly at the dregs of his pint. 'I should have done that when we first met but I hadn't the neck, and now it's too late. He's wearing me down.'

'Cheer up, for God's sake, you're depressing me so much I'll have to get you another pint.'

Three hours later, flushed with Guinness, we found the evening sun blinding after the dim light in the bar. Ominous rumbles reminded us that it was time that we ate. Laden with supplies, we still sweated as we made our way up the steep hill back to the bay and our dinghy. Once we were afloat with the shopping stowed in the bow, I opted to row and the other two happily agreed and sprawled fore and aft, watching with critical eyes. Gerard trailed a hand in the water. He had pushed his duncher back to splash water on his brow, revealing a neat white line around his forehead. His deeply tanned face was topped by a balding egg-white patch. I laughed.

'What are you cackling at? Your own mug looks like the setting sun,' he growled, pushing his duncher back in place.

I settled into a steady rhythm at the oars, leaving a trail of bubbles in our wake. Behind us the headland slipped away as the harbour, which I could glimpse over my right shoulder, slowly got nearer. My arms were beginning to

feel a bit leaden but I was chuffed at accomplishing a long straight row on my own.

'I went into the post office but there was no mail for us,' said Gerard.

George wanted to know how often he called.

'Once or twice a week, but the islanders would bring any mail over if they saw it there. Sometimes it's a fortnight before any arrives, then I get three or four letters in one day.'

I negotiated the harbour entrance without mishap. My first trip, I thought, as the keel grated on the sand. The first of many, and not just in the day but after dark as well.

That day established the pattern for a routine, and often I was out sketching long before the others were awake. My belly always drew me back for lunch and then I was off again until teatime, and sometimes after the evening meal as well. Rowing to Roundstone for food was the only variation in the routine. There were times when George got quite angry about it.

'Why can't you sit on your arse and relax like the rest of us?' he would demand.

'What happens if it rains tomorrow?' I'd reply. 'I could be stuck inside for a week. I don't want to waste time when the weather is good.'

Although there was no way of knowing it at the time, the weather for most of our stay was idyllic; blue skies every morning, constant sunshine roasting our skulls – with the exception of a spectacular few days (of which more later).

However, George's complaints upset me, until one evening Gerard confided, 'He doesn't like to think that you are doing more work than him. You're giving him a guilty conscience. The idea that anyone should work harder at painting than he does annoys him.'

I was flattered at the very notion that I could produce more work than George, as he was prolific, but I was learning from these two, listening and watching everything that was said and done.

On the island Gerard was the man in charge. Under his instruction we each chipped in fifteen shillings a week to the kitty for food – any extras such as sweets, smokes, booze, had to come out of our own pockets. With the cottage came the use of the two boats: the currach, which could take four people, and a dinghy which took three. The currach worried George. Not its buoyancy – that had been proven on our arrival with the four of us and our luggage aboard. But what would keep it afloat, he wanted to know, if it was overturned and holed? At least the dinghy would float. He never seemed to wonder just how long we might have to cling to it before anyone noticed the half-submerged hull.

It was easy launching the boats at high tide. You could get in off the beach or you could tow the boat along to the steps in the harbour wall. At low tide it was different as a mass of rocks was exposed. Then it was hard work, risking damage to either limbs or dignity before we could get the boats into water deep enough to float with us on board. It took only a couple of disasters that left us with wet feet and legs and much profanity for us to decide that we would only launch at low tide in an emergency.

Landing was no better. We arrived back one evening after lingering longer than we intended in O'Dowd's pub to find the tide well out beyond the harbour entrance. Weed-covered rocks glinted under a crescent moon. Long shadows hid little pools and deep crevices. The thought of hauling the dinghy across this minefield was daunting but it had to be done. We cursed between grunts as we slipped and stumbled, our trousers soaked. However, we got nothing worse than a wetting before we felt soft sand under our boots. We had learnt our lesson. Next morning our boots and trousers had to be left to dry in the sun before they could be worn again. We soon became expert at judging how deep the water might be three or four hours ahead. We swore never to launch or arrive again at low tide. Desert islands have their disadvantages.

On my second morning on the island I set off alone to explore the ruined cottages standing beside a deserted beach. I was hoping that they would inspire some better pictures. So far, my watercolour paintings had not been very successful. I was so absorbed in my work that the morning and afternoon flew. By teatime I packed up for the day, still not satisfied with my efforts. Tomorrow I would start all over again.

I decided to go back to the ruined cottages after tea, their empty windows staring out at the endless sea. Not a single piece of timber remained in them. Some stones had collapsed onto the floors but the chimney breasts were intact. I peered up the soot-blackened stonework at a patch of blue sky peeping at me as though from the end of a black tunnel. I examined the threshold where cement-filled cavities that levelled the stonework to take the door frame had gaps eaten into them by time and weather. I wondered what expectations, joys

George and Gerard (sitting) with some of the islanders

and calamities had been experienced by the family that had lived there. I had to admire whoever had built these cottages. Some of the boulders in the walls must have taken three men to lift. I marvelled at the way the lattice of the stone had been put together. There had been no concrete blocks and cement mixers here.

A sadness slept around these ruins that I did not care to take to bed with me, so I kept going along the path. A donkey stuck his head over the wall, but as I leaned over to pat him, he galloped away up the field. Heads suddenly popped up among the boulders. Three small children emerged, heads lowered, hands tucked behind them, staring at me.

'Hello, what's your names?' I asked.

Shy smiles and silence was all I got before they raced off giggling and disappeared behind an outhouse.

Making my way back an hour later, I was met by the strains of 'The Wild Colonial Boy' accompanying a voice singing at full blast. Gerard was feeling the joy of life. George and he were sitting outside the cottage, with a black gramophone perched on a wooden box beside the door. The lid was open, the shiny chromium head wobbling up and down as it ground out the last few bars. Bottles of Guinness stood between their outstretched legs. The silence returned as the tune died away. On the windowsill Suzy Blue Hole sat hunched up, her feet tucked out of sight beneath her.

'I could hear your melodious voice halfway across the island,' I said, taking a seat beside Gerard.

'Is that what you call it?' said George.

Gerard wound up the gramophone, fitted a new needle, and blew the dust off another record before putting it on the turntable. A tinny-sounding, scratched version of 'Danny Boy' sung by Count John McCormack issued forth.

George pulled a face. 'Play something else. That sounds bloody awful.'

Gerard ignored him, letting the record run to the end before he carefully restored it to its cardboard cover. 'Great record, I love it.'

'Where did you disappear to?' George asked, eyeing me.

Filling my cherrywood pipe, I told him I'd been looking at the derelict cottages and planned to draw them tomorrow morning. Blue smoke drifted sideways round the corner, drawing my eyes to an islander silhouetted against

the skyline who was prodding home his cow with an excited dog yapping in attendance. They slowly disappeared behind a rise. Dusk began to fall but it was still warm as we sat talking in the gathering gloom. Sheep settled down on the hillsides and the house lights in Roundstone glittered like bright yellow stars against the loom of the mainland.

When we finally moved indoors and lit the lamps I felt as though my arms and legs were dropping off and I needed a match to prop my eyelids open. My sunburnt face matched the red of the fire and I began to doze, my head drooping to one side. It seemed like hours, but was probably only a few minutes, before George jolted me awake by kicking the chair leg.

'Away to your beddies. You're making me tired just sitting here watching you.'

Forcing my eyes open, I mumbled an apology before dragging myself off to bed.

'Christ, I've never met anyone like him! I know nobody else who falls asleep like that on the dot.'

These were the last words I heard as sleep claimed me after a long working day on Inishlacken. There were many more of these to come.

2

Our days on the island were so alike, our daily pattern of work so similar, that I found it hard to believe that we had been there a week. We awoke each morning to a blue sky dappled with puffs of cotton-wool clouds drifting to the horizon and constant sunshine that turned my complexion a more fiery hue each day. The skin peeled off my nose in strips and my forehead glowed like a bonfire.

One day, sitting in the shadow of a large rock, I sketched an islander slowly clipping the wool from the belly of a sheep, using a huge pair of scissors. The sheep lay sideways, its feet bound with a piece of rope, as its winter overcoat was removed. Once scalped and untethered, it swayed upright and bounded off in leaps. I finished the drawing, turned to a new page, and swiftly brushed in a sketch of the old man puffing his pipe, his head wreathed in smoke.

'Can I have a likeness of meself when ye've done?' he asked.

'Sure you can. Have this one,' I said, tearing out the page.

'Do I look like that?' A smile broadened his face as he looked intently at the sketch. 'The wife will have it hanging over the fireplace in no time at all,' he chuckled.

I told him I'd be back after dinner and we'd have a go at another one.

I climbed the stone wall skirting the path to head back towards our cottage. We had decided that our main meal of the day would be cooked on a rota basis, the duty cook serving up whatever took his fancy. Usually it was spuds dished up with something fried or stewed, although Gerard's meals were more adventurous than the offerings presented by either George or me. Having lived by himself for years, he had had more practice. I always knew when it was his turn by the delicious smells that used to permeate the cottage, causing my tongue to hang out in anticipation. It was George's turn today. His cooking, like mine, was very basic. There was no sign of him, no smell of cooking. Through the door I could see Gerard sitting painting by his easel, so engrossed that he was unaware of my arrival. I startled him.

'Where's George? He's not even peeled the spuds yet. I'm starving.'

'You always are. I haven't clapped eyes on him all morning. God knows where he's got to,' Gerard muttered, leaving aside his brushes.

'Doesn't he know he's cooking today? It's going to be teatime before we get our dinner. He sits up half the night reading, can't get out of bed in the morning, and he's never hungry when we are,' I exploded.

'Never worry yourself, a good feed will be waiting for you tonight. We're going to Kate O'Brien's. She sets up a feed fit for a lord,' Gerard said as he started washing his brushes in turpentine.

'Well, I'll have to make do with bread and cheese,' I grumbled. 'God knows where the wee skitter is, but no doubt he'll come up with some plausible excuse.'

Gerard bent over the glass sheet he used as a palette, scraping off crusted paint with a knife. 'It makes a better palette than wood any day,' he told me. Clipped to his easel were three ink sketches of Roundstone which he had used as the basis for his painting. It was a view over the harbour, looking up the

main street. White houses humped up the hill towards a bright blue sky, fishermen bent over their nets and a large seagull occupied the foreground.

'How are you getting on with the oil?' I asked.

'It's a bit early to say. But it looks promising so far. I like it.'

Paintings were rarely finished in one session, usually taking two or three overpaintings.

'Hand me that tin of whitening and a brush,' he said, pointing to a tin of primer. He had dropped to his knees on the floor, where a sheet of paper had been laid across the tiles with two boards ready for priming on top.

'How many coats do you give them?' I asked.

'Three.'

'Good God, that's a lot of priming.'

'Whoever invented hardboard should have got a medal,' said Gerard, carefully feathering away his brush marks.

'I hope he got two – he deserved it,' I answered, handing him another board to prime with white paint.

Before the arrival of hardboard, artists had had to make use of a variety of surfaces on which to paint, their choice being strongly dependent on how well off they were. In our case money problems bedevilled our lives and apart from the difficulty of finding enough of it to provide food and shelter, we had the additional quandary of funding supplies of painting materials. The stretched canvases sold in art shops were out of our reach. So we improvised. Wood panels, plywood and even the backs of hard-bound books were all pressed into service. We used

Island People by Gerard Dillon

to haunt Belfast's old Smithfield Market searching for large hard-backed tomes, preferably with illustrations on good-quality art paper, the reverse side of which made an excellent surface for pen and ink drawings. The hard covers were peeled of their paper backing, stripped to bare cardboard, then sized and primed to make them ready to use for oil paintings. At one time George became enthusiastic about using the plywood from dismantled tea chests and was only discouraged when Gerard pointed out to him the risk of his paintings being lost to posterity by the depredation of woodworms.

Coat canvas was another cheap answer. This was a coarse-weave canvas used for stiffening the lining of jackets and was bought by the yard from garment makers. However, this had one big disadvantage. Despite repeated applications of glue sizing, the white primer would penetrate the coarse weave and we spent as much time treating the back of the material as we did the front.

George, never the most patient of men, was much vexed by these procedures and used to rant about the amount of time he had to spend priming his canvases. As well as this, he was completely useless at making the wooden frames which, with tiny tacks, were used to hold the canvases taut. He banged his fingers as often as he did the tin tacks. Eventually, after one painful episode, he decided that he was no carpenter and resorted to heavy cardboard again. Smithfield's junk shops were also a source of old gilded frames in all shapes and sizes. We used to poke and rummage in our search for some that would stand scumbling and overpainting. I remember the odd looks I got from other passengers as I sat on the tram with two or three battered frames jammed between my knees.

Then, seemingly overnight, our deliverance arrived in the form of a Swedish invention called hardboard. It was rigid, easily cut (being a quarter the thickness of a stretcher and canvas), and not prone to the dents, hollows and accidental holes that disfigured our canvases. And best of all, woodworms found it impenetrable. For the times, it was expensive but far less so than canvas. Five shillings – twenty-five pence in today's money – would buy a square foot of it, but the shopkeepers would cut any length that was required.

One day I discovered Gerard in his back yard, fanning one of his hardboard paintings with a blowtorch.

'What are you doing now?' I asked, watching the tight, blackened curls of paint peeling off the board.

'Took a scunner at it. I couldn't stand the sight of it any longer,' he answered as the blue flame of the blowlamp cleaned off the last of the paint.

I stood in silence, mesmerised by the idea of scrubbing a duff painting and reusing the board. I was utterly sold on the merits of this new invention and have found that paintings executed on hardboard show no signs of cracking or flaking paint even fifty years later.

Gerard had the second board half-primed when he suddenly stopped with the brush poised in mid-air. 'Look what's coming at last.'

George's head and shoulders were just visible beyond the stone wall as he plodded toward us. He climbed up the path, his drawing equipment tucked under his arm.

'Well, wherever he's been doing whatever it is, he's still walking,' said Gerard.

I think he genuinely worried about some physical mishap befalling us. George and I had both noticed how much he fretted when either of us failed to appear at the expected time.

George arrived at the door puffing hard, sweating and complaining that he was suffering from heat exhaustion. He dropped his sketch pad on the floor, ditching himself full length on Gerard's bed.

'Where the hell have you been all this time?' demanded Gerard. 'We were thinking of sending out a search party.'

'Old Séamus invited me into his cottage. You know what he's like. I couldn't get away, and anyway the crack was good. He was telling me about the time

he worked in the steel mills in Pittsburgh.' He had got his breath and lit a cigarette. Old Séamus

'Christ, I've heard that story about fifty times,' Gerard laughed as he stacked his primed boards against the wall.

Séamus was over seventy. His legs were a bit shaky but he staggered across to the cottage most mornings to take a seat at the door, a cigarette and a mug of tea. Despite his age, he still stood well over six feet tall, and in his prime he must have been as well-muscled as an ox. His dress never varied: a lumberjack's peaked cap with buttoned-up ear flaps and a thick woollen tartan jacket with deep pockets. The heat on the seat might be blistering but Séamus always wore that jacket with the collar buttoned up to the neck as if a Force 10 gale was blowing in from the sea. He lived alone so he was probably glad of the company and the crack was enjoyed by all of us. He made a wonderful model. We all drew him.

'Never mind about Séamus, what about our dinner?' Gerard rebuked him with a sideways glance at me. 'MacIntyre's dying of hunger, although he's just had a bap and cheese.'

'He's always bloody hungry even though he eats twice as much as we do,' growled George, his hackles rising.

'Next time we cook, your plate will be empty if you forget us again,' promised Gerard.

'Aw, quit narking. The pair of you are going on as if you haven't had a meal

Main Street, Roundstone

for a month.' Filling a saucepan with water from the black kettle, he said, 'I'll boil some eggs and make toast to go with them.'

'Christ, you make them sound so exciting.' Gerard rolled his eyes at me. 'I'm slabbering at the mouth at the very thought.'

As we ate, Gerard and I dithered about whether or not we should use the currach for our evening trip to Roundstone. The previous day we had made a trial run in it beyond the harbour. As it was so much lighter, it shot through the water far faster than the dinghy. I had had problems with the fixed oars but had soon got the hang of them. By the time we were done, Gerard and I were rowing like veterans. We had tried to persuade George to accompany us but he would have none of it. He was still unhappy when we came ashore.

'The dinghy might be on the heavy side but it will take a knock or the odd bump with no more harm than a dinge in the paint,' he said. And then, tapping the thin skin of the currach with his toe, 'Scratch that thing on a mussel bed and it will sink like a stone.' George's obvious lack of enthusiasm and the prospect of a late-night crossing with the crew possibly in an unseaman-like condition persuaded us, in the end, in favour of taking the dinghy.

It was about eight o'clock that evening when we beached the boat and set off along the road to Roundstone. The evening sun was dazzling as we plodded up the brow of the hill disturbing the crows strutting across the road looking for titbits. They waited until the last minute before flapping off in slow motion,

cawing their disapproval at our intrusion. The main street was empty as we strolled through the village, only a couple of bicycles propped outside Connolly's bar hinting at life behind the doors.

Kate O'Brien's house sat among trees on a bend in the road about half a mile beyond the harbour. We entered through a tall gate a well-tended garden with a smooth lawn which faced an imposing cream-painted house. A menagerie of cats in shades of black, brown and white stopped chasing their tails through the shrubbery to stare at the three strangers crunching up the gravelled drive. Our hostess was waiting and rose to greet us from a white garden seat near the front door. She wore a long black dress that rustled in the still evening. I hung back when Gerard began the introductions. It was the first time I had ever been in such a large house, one so well-proportioned and furnished with taste and wealth. I was overawed.

I remembered all too well the daft comments I had made in the past when in strange company and how the recipients had stared back blankly at me, wondering what I was talking about. So my inclination now was to listen, watch and to try to avoid getting involved in a conversation that might end up with me having to advance an opinion on some subject of which I was completely ignorant. I would let the other two make the running. They would not require any prompting.

I had imagined that anyone who lived in a house of this size and elegance would be aloof and distant with the likes of us, but Kate O'Brien greeted us warmly and with such friendliness that I forgot my good intentions and was soon babbling away. Her name had meant nothing to me but Gerard had quickly dispelled my ignorance of this much-admired Irish novelist and insisted that I should not feel embarrassed at not having read one of her books. Before the evening was over I was promising myself a visit to the local library when I got back to Belfast.

'Shall I call you Jim or James?' she asked as we shook hands.

'I answer to either,' I replied, trying to hide my shyness.

'I like James best, it's much more dignified. I hope these two are treating you well on the island.'

'Well, they let me row the boat across every time and then carry the groceries from Roundstone to the boat and up from the harbour to the cottage.'

'Gentlemen, I'm surprised that two worthies like you should take such blatant advantage of this young man.'

The two worthies nudged each other.

'Take no notice of him, Kate. He's taking the mickey, having a joke at our expense. He likes rowing so we encourage him to practise it,' said Gerard. 'Anyway, the exercise is good for him. It's making him very fit – and look at his glorious suntan.'

I could have killed him, for although the tan was hiding my blushes, I was suddenly reminded that my peeling nose seemed to glow more brightly after sundown.

Through a wide-panelled door we entered a high-ceilinged room with alabaster cornices and an ornamental centre rose which supported an enormous etched-glass light fitting. Heavy leather chairs sat on a multi-coloured carpet and the walls were hung with paintings, mostly oils. Through the windows a breathtaking view encompassed Roundstone Bay and far beyond.

'Come,' said Kate, 'make yourselves comfortable. What can I get you to drink?'

George asked for a Guinness and Gerard a whiskey. I dithered until Kate suggested I try the whiskey. A few years earlier in Belfast, George had introduced me to my first pint of Guinness one sunny lunchtime in the Washington bar in Howard Street, but although the bitter taste had put me off at first, I had persevered. However, whiskey was a new experience. A heavy cut-glass tumbler, half-filled with Power's whiskey, the amber glow reflected from every facet, was set before me. The glass was like a lead weight as I took a tentative sip. It slid like red-hot lava straight down to the pit of my stomach. I gasped and struggled for breath.

'God,' I whispered hoarsely, 'is all whiskey as strong as this?'

'Quite right, James,' beamed Kate. 'Never drink Scotch; it is too bland. I knew you would like it.'

Gerard, grinning, handed me a jug of water and advised me to damp it down a bit. After a few more sips a pleasant glow began to spread inside me and as I listened to the boisterous laughter of my companions, I had the impression that they were even more gregarious than usual. Art, books, music and scandal were discussed and elaborated upon; scorn was poured, praise heaped, no one and nothing escaped the wide-ranging opinions offered, considered and disposed of.

My glass was refilled several times; it did not feel so heavy now. As I moved to add a drop of water to it, a slight unsteadiness swayed me from one leg to the other. I blinked. Again, I could have sworn that the glass moved. It had. Next time my left hand anchored it as I poured the water; a little went into the glass, the rest onto the polished table as the tumbler moved again.

'Here, give me that jug a minute,' whispered Gerard. 'Don't drink any more of that stuff tonight. You have to row us home, remember.'

I did as he told me, nursing my drink, although I was now finding it very pleasant. I tried to keep abreast of the conversation but my concentration began to drift and my head to droop. I had to jerk it upright in a barrage of blinks.

A hand was placed on my shoulder and Kate's voice said that she thought young James would welcome a sandwich. 'There's chicken, salmon, cheese and ham. Tuck in, I want to see nothing but empty plates when you leave.'

I thought the whiskey had fuddled my hearing. My ma did not believe in wasting good money on luxuries such as chicken and salmon; she bought good plain stuff to fill the belly. We moved into the dining room. A large table was littered with plates of sandwiches, an apple tart as big as a cartwheel and a

massive chocolate cake. I blinked at the sight, my eyes automatically searching for those chicken and salmon treats. I had to force myself to hold back, to be polite and let the others start first. Whether it was the whiskey, my perpetually empty stomach or the excitement of the evening, I do not know, but everything edible on that table disappeared like snow in summer. Gerard belched and hastily excused himself.

'The Arabs say that belching is the way to show appreciation of a good meal,' said Kate with a smile.

Later, sprawled in an armchair, I declined any more whiskey. The sandwiches had stopped my head spinning but I decided to stick to lemonade for the rest of the evening. I had to get these two fools home. From the way they were behaving they were going to need me and a bit of luck.

Kate asked if I had any plans for an exhibition. I had, but not for a little while. It would be a collection of drawings made around Inishlacken and Roundstone. She said she would like to see some of the drawings and I promised to bring them on our next visit. She would not be drawn on her latest book, admitting only that it was a historical novel. I remembered old W.R. Gordon in Belfast asking me to look up his friend Bulmer Hobson so I asked Kate if she knew of him. She told me that half the country knew him. He was a great nationalist and had been involved in the 1916 rising. He lived on the other side of town and anyone could show me his house. A great nationalist? I wondered how W.R. Gordon had got to know him. He sounded as though he would be worth a visit.

The pleasant evening passed in a flash but there were problems ahead – like getting into Inishlacken harbour before it dried out. We had previously agreed midnight as the deadline and time was getting on. My companions, enjoying themselves enormously and totally inebriated, told me to stop spoiling the evening. We had plenty of time, they said. After two further vain attempts to get them to move, Kate intervened, cajoling them with a promise of another evening soon. They drained their glasses reluctantly and headed for the door crabwise, giving the furniture a wide berth. We bid Kate farewell, thanking her for her hospitality and a wonderful time, and ambled noisily down the gravelled drive.

It was a dark starlit night. Very dark. The lamp outside the front door illuminated only the steps. Then we were on our own with nothing but the wan light from a sliver of moon dribbling through the canopy of branches. There was no noise, no motor cars, no people or traffic of any kind. Raising my wrist, I could just about make out the hands of my watch. It was 12.30 a.m. – we had to hurry if we were to make the tide. We moved on, our footsteps indecently loud on the gravel, into the darkness hiding those big ornamental iron gates. Gerard found them first, crashing headlong into them and staggering backwards before collapsing into dense shrubbery, leaving only his legs spreadeagled on the path.

'He's drunk as a lord,' muttered George.

We laughed, not realising what had happened. Then the panic bells rang as the shrubbery remained motionless and George and I had to grope in the darkness for the body.

Suddenly, in a noisy clatter of breaking branches, Gerard emerged and staggered onto the path. 'What hit me?'

George realised what had happened. 'You bloody eejit,' he yelled, 'the gate was closed. Are you all right? Did you hurt yourself?'

'Naw, I'm all right, just banged my knee.'

Gerard tried to stand on one leg while he tenderly felt the other. He fell over again. We waited as he pulled himself upright and brushed himself down, all the while assuring us that it was a good thing he had been drunk when he fell as, otherwise, his abrupt descent into the undergrowth would have ended with a slow ride to Clifden hospital, his reasoning being that his state of inebriation had relaxed him so much that he had come to no harm.

We eventually got through the gate onto the road, clanging it shut again and disturbing the bats flitting at high speed through the maze of branches. As we moved out from under the shelter of the trees I picked up three pebbles.

'Wait till you see this,' I said.

One after another I threw the pebbles straight up over the sea wall. A squadron of bats appeared from nowhere, hurtling after the stones, zooming skywards just before they splashed into the water.

'Where did you learn that trick?' asked George.

'From my grandfather.'

Seconds later they were both throwing stones into the air with all the enthusiasm of kids throwing balls at a coconut shy. The pair of them were in good cheer as they lurched down the centre of the road to Roundstone. I was the sober one. I had to get us back to Inishlacken. The noise of their voices and laughter carried far into the quiet, still night. I was worried that some irate locals would fling open their bedroom windows and tell them to shut up. A dog barked and was joined by another and I begged them to lower their voices as we got to the harbour square. I was told to get stuffed. A single light burnt bright on a pedestal high over the harbour wall to guide home the fishermen. Behind us, the town was in darkness. There were no street lights, and drawn blinds hid the windows, although up on the hill a solitary yellow spark was a reminder that someone was having a restless night.

It was now one o'clock in the morning and I could see by the light of the beacon that the tide was on the ebb. I tried to shut out of my mind the picture of George and Gerard in their present state staggering over the boulder-strewn harbour entrance on Inishlacken in the darkness. I tried to hurry them on. However, nothing I said had any effect and we sounded like an army on the march as the houses hemming the road magnified the clatter of our boots on the rough tarmac. I strode ahead, anxious to get to the beach and the waiting dinghy.

It was not easy hauling the dinghy single-handed across the beach toward the receding sea but I managed it with the mooring rope over my shoulder. I sat down in the bow to get my breath back as I waited for the other two.

Across the water Inishlacken was a black mass huddled against a luminous sky, and I was confident that by following the beach round I could find the harbour. I would see the silhouette of the schoolhouse and it would make a good signpost. I heard their two voices across the dunes.

'Will you hurry up,' I yelled. 'We'll be bloody lucky if we don't wreck the boat getting it into the harbour.'

'Aw, shut your noise, there'll be plenty of water left to float us in,' replied Gerard with alcoholic optimism.

'I just hope you're right. If I hold the boat against that rock, do you think you can get in without capsizing it?' I growled.

George cast a timid leg over the side and he made it safely to the stern. Gerard got his feet wrong, rocking the dinghy violently, as he put all his weight on one side. For the second time that evening he tumbled over backwards, landing with a thud on the floorboards with his legs hanging over the centre thwart.

'Christ, he's going to kill himself or drown the lot of us,' George wailed.

Gerard lay on his back giggling until George hauled him upright by the collar of his jacket. I could not help. I needed both hands to hold the dinghy and to make sure I did not fall in as the boat swayed away from me.

'You bloody eejits. The three of us could have ended up in the tide' – I pointed to George – 'and he'd have gone down like a stone – he can't swim!'

I could not see the look on their faces in the darkness but my protestations must have sobered them momentarily because I was able to start rowing without further argument. Not for long, however. A hundred yards offshore the banter restarted as they recovered their nerve and the use of their vocal chords; this time it was about my unwillingness to engage wholeheartedly in the various arguments that had gone on during the evening.

'Listen, you two, even if I had wanted to join in, I couldn't have got a word in edgeways. I just couldn't compete with a couple of egotists of your standing. You really excelled yourselves tonight. Anyway, I much prefer listening to a couple of argumentative sods like you two sounding off.'

That caused a gale of raucous laughter as I bent my back to the oars.

'Tell me, what did you think of Kate O'Brien?' enquired Gerard.

'I liked her. Mind, I liked her house even better. One of those rooms would make a great studio,' I grunted between strokes. 'I'll have to get something for my nose in Roundstone tomorrow. I caught her staring at it a couple of times tonight. It's like a beacon and it's sore as well as peeling.'

They digested this in silence for a minute.

'Staring at you, you say,' said George.

'At my nose,' I replied.

'Well, I reckon she fancies you, nose and all,' Gerard said with rising enthusiasm. 'A virile young fella like you, full of beans, and artistic as well. I think you've made a mark there.'

'Don't be so bloody daft, she's old enough to be my granny,' I said, feeling my cheeks burning at the very idea and glad of the darkness that hid my embarrassment.

They started cackling again.

'I think he really bowled her over,' said George.

'Will you knock it off. Any more talk like that and you can row yourselves home.'

Gerard took no notice. 'Did you hear him say how much he liked her house? God, but he's the fly boy. I bet you he's planning another late night there on his own without a word to us. It won't upset us, George,' he went on, 'if he gets himself installed there, we could visit them. I'll bet the beds are really soft and luxurious, not like the straw and horse hair we sleep on.'

'And she's well-heeled – he wouldn't have to do another hand's turn for the rest of his life,' George quipped.

'Aye, and think of the stories we could tell about him in Belfast and Dublin. We'd get free drinks for years. Young artist sets up house with well-known novelist Kate O'Brien,' Gerard went on eagerly.

Here we go again, I thought, trying to ignore them and concentrate on my rowing. They enjoyed taking the mickey out of me, or anyone else for that matter. It was their favourite pastime. Each vying to outdo the other in outlandish verbal concoctions in which the earthier the subject the more extravagant their inventiveness. They usually ended with a poem, each one adding a line at a time, the whole punctuated with hoots of laughter. Nothing and no one was sacred. Take Nano Reid, a Drogheda artist. She had written to Gerard to say that she would be on Inishlacken in July, recent surgery for haemorrhoids having prevented her from getting there any earlier, and warning against the consequences of sitting on damp stone walls. If poor Nano had heard the ribald comments that the news of her affliction precipitated, she would have banned the two of them from her acquaintance for ever.

However, just at the moment, I had other things on my mind than their bawdy accompaniment to my rowing. The slap of water on rocks was a comforting and welcome sound. It meant that there still was water in the harbour and we were nearly home.

Gerard saw the moonlit island first. He stretched, causing the boat to pitch violently. 'Thank God, we're almost there. I'm ready for a sleep,' he yawned.

'Stop rocking the boat, we're not home and dry yet,' I yelled in my best Captain Bligh manner. 'I can't see how much water there is in the harbour.'

The long harbour wall loomed up, black and menacing, the rocks spread along the face hiding the entrance. Then the glint of moonlight on water beyond them betrayed a gap.

'Take it easy, Jim.' George was suddenly apprehensive.

The black water looked very deep. I swung the dinghy round, keeping my eye on the sharp outline of the harbour entrance. As we crept closer, the oars snagged seaweed and an ominous bump shuddered us aside.

'Watch what you're doing – we'll hit a rock,' shouted George in panic.

The keel swung clear and I knew that we had bumped into a rock alongside the channel. Confidently, I turned the dinghy around and into the horseshoe entrance. The harbour was almost, but not quite, dry. We would have to splash through scattered stones and seaweed to reach the beach, but we had accomplished our first night-time crossing. Thank heaven God looks after drunks and fools.

Manhandling the boat up the beach sobered George and Gerard, although judging from the way they staggered up to the cottage, I thought that they would have the mother of all hangovers in the morning. We were too tired to talk any more, and flopping onto our beds, we dropped like stones into slumber.

Next morning the chatter of the island children as they trooped past the cottage on their way to board the currach that ferried them to school on the mainland told me that we had overslept. The cottage was silent – very silent. I poked my head round the bedroom door. Gerard was in a restless sleep, with a basin on the floor beside him. I dressed quietly, tiptoeing around as softly as possible to avoid waking him. Halfway through my toast, I heard a groan and the creak of bedsprings. Gerard opened one bleary eye. He closed it quickly.

'Are you all right?' I asked.

'Jesus, I'm dying. My guts are killing me. I thought I'd die in the night, and you two were snoring your heads off.'

'Serves you right. You nearly drowned us with your antics in the boat and you drank enough to float us across and back again,' I said unsympathetically. Then I asked him if he'd like a cup of tea.

Gerard helping with the school run

'Oh no! I couldn't face anything. Open that cupboard and get me a spoonful of milk of magnesia to damp down these guts of mine.'

I lifted the blue bottle from the shelf. It was empty, although I shook it vigorously to make sure. Gerard groaned as he turned onto his side.

George appeared about an hour later, apparently none the worse for the booze he had drunk. He enquired what was up with Gerard, as we gazed solemnly at the heap of bedclothes with just the tip of a bald head showing.

'You know he has an ulcer – he shouldn't have drunk all that whiskey last night,' George said.

'He wants milk of magnesia,' I said, 'but the bottle is empty. I think we should row over to Roundstone and get some. Look at the colour of him. That wall looks healthier than he does.'

George shook his head, agreeing that Gerard would not be worth a damn all day but he did not think we should leave him alone.

It was a glorious morning. George and I sprawled in the sun, saying little, unwilling to break the peace and mindful of Gerard twitching in pain under the bedclothes. We dozed, a dog barked nearby, and turf smoke drifted lazily up, scenting the air. Suzy Blue Hole suddenly appeared, tail swishing, ears cocked, watching something on the path skirting the cottage. She crouched, stiffened and bolted towards the rocks behind our turf shed. Someone or something was coming. The clatter of a walking stick announced the arrival, long before we caught sight of him, of old Séamus. He settled himself in the sun while we told him about Gerard's indisposition.

'Ach, many's the morning I felt like that when I was in the steel mills but I couldn't afford to lie in bed. I just had to get on with it.' His craggy face split in a nostalgic smile. 'Ye always swear by all that's holy that ye'll never touch another drop,' he laughed, 'but I tell ye, that's one lesson ye never learn.'

We gave him a mug of tea and a biscuit to encourage him to chat about Inishlacken and its people, past and present.

'I hear the lads are going shark fishing tomorrow,' he volunteered.

George leaned forward apprehensively. 'Shark fishing? Where do they go to find sharks?'

Séamus pointed out to sea, swinging his arm in a semi-circle around the horizon. 'Out there, in those waters. They're contrary buggers. When they take a notion they come in very close.' His Adam's apple rose as he gulped his tea.

George slumped back, trying to think of something to say and looking like a man who had just heard something he did not want to know about.

Séamus drained his tea. 'Ye can never tell when ye'll see them,' he said. 'There's times they roam up and down the length of this coast.'

George looked unhappy.

Half an hour later, going on for dinnertime, Séamus heaved himself off the bench, ran a hand across his bushy moustache, took a quick look at Gerard's recumbent form and departed, shaking his head sadly at the inability of artists to hold their liquor like steel men.

By now we were beginning to feel worried about Gerard. He still lay, huddled up in bed, with his face to the wall and showing no sign of improvement.

'You stay with him and I'll row across to Roundstone for a bottle of milk of magnesia,' I said to George. 'He should look better than he does by now. I'll get some bread and cheese while I'm there.'

George took an anxious look round the door. 'He's not great. I hope to God he's more lively by teatime. You'd think the eejit would have kept a spare bottle of magnesia. He knows what whiskey does to him.'

An hour later I was on the main street in Roundstone, passing the time of day with a shopkeeper. I swear a knowing look flitted across her face when I asked for the milk of magnesia.

'Would it be for yourself?' she asked.

I told her it was for Gerard as he was feeling a bit under the weather.

'Has he eaten something that disagreed with him – or is it the drink?' she asked, fixing me with a sharp eye.

I did not want to discuss the subject and mumbled that I thought it might be a bit of both. She tut-tutted to herself as she wrapped my purchases, commenting that we must have had a very late night. I pretended to examine the stacks of tins on the shelves while I wondered how she knew. Had she

heard the racket we made last night? Had someone told her where we had been, or was she just fishing? I should have guessed, of course, that everyone in Roundstone would have known exactly what we were doing. News of our escapade must have done the rounds like wildfire.

'We spent the evening at Kate O'Brien's. The crack was good and we were late getting away and then we slept in this morning.' I edged out of the shop, saying goodbye as I went.

'Well, I hope Gerard will be better soon. Tell him I was asking for him,' she called after me.

I put my back into my rowing, the oars creaking as the water sprayed over the bows. It was hard work but I enjoyed it, with the magnificent seascape all around me, plate-sized jellyfish floating by and the ever-present smell of the sea and the boat. But the thought of Gerard nagged me on. I ought to have enquired about a doctor in Roundstone, I thought. Stomach ulcers could be serious and if they bled, very serious. This time there was no difficulty in negotiating the harbour. The tide was in. I pulled the dinghy hard onto the beach, hauling it clear of the high-water mark. Our blue door was open as I approached the cottage, but I could see no sign of life except for Suzy Blue Hole sitting on the windowsill, staring at me. I walked quickly up the path, dreading what I might find when I reached the door.

George was reading by the turf fire and Gerard was propped up in bed with a mug of tea held in both hands. I sighed with relief to see him sitting up.

'What's this then?' I asked. 'Me blistering my hands to get to Roundstone for your bloody medicine while there you are, sitting swigging mugs of tea. You must be feeling better.'

Actually, I thought that he looked like a ghost warmed up, but a semblance of his old grin spread across his face as he replied that he was feeling a bit better. I told him he'd looked terrible when I left.

'And that's how I feel now, but it's not so bad.' He took the bottle of milk of magnesia from me.

'Get a couple of spoonfuls of that inside you and make sure you keep a spare bottle for next time.'

'I never want to drink again. That was the last time. I've finished with it for life,' answered Gerard feelingly.

The bright orange sun had slipped below the horizon before Gerard eventually left his bed. George and I had propped ourselves against the harbour wall to watch one of the islanders sewing up a hole in a fishing net. We heard his footsteps behind us. His duncher was pulled low over his eyes and his hands were buried deep in his trouser pockets. A wan, sheepish grin lifted his moustache at the corners as he took a seat beside us.

'Are you going to make it?' George asked.

Gerard skimmed a stone across the water, causing rings of ripples to wash against the sand. He was smiling. 'I'll survive.'

3

With one exception, none of the animals kept by the people of Inishlacken bothered us. Cows, goats and hens lived a docile life within the confines of their stone walls. The exception was the geese; they were holy terrors, shattering our nerves and causing us to skulk behind walls, never knowing when they were going to strike next. A gaggle of them lived barely three hundred yards behind our cottage in an outhouse belonging to another cottage close to the path by the beach, a path we had to take, as our eggs were supplied by the owner of the recalcitrant birds. The only alternative was to make a detour round the island, which involved the scaling of innumerable stone walls.

One morning when the dew had barely gone, George and I went sketching. He followed the stony path by the cottage while I found a seat behind a stone wall up on a hilll. Before I could get started, the tranquillity of the morning was suddenly ruptured by a loud and raucous honking accompanied by the beating of wings, the pounding of feet and a stream of colourful obscenities. George suddenly appeared, galloping like a madman, arms clawing for the sky, desperately trying to keep ahead of an irate goose which pursued him with beating wings and neck outstretched like a battering ram, its webbed feet barely touching the ground and honking furiously as it went. For a moment I was transfixed with astonishment, but as George gained the high ground and collapsed flat on his back beside me, I exploded with laughter, the tears running down my cheeks.

'Jesus,' gasped George between gulps of air, 'I thought I was a gonner that time.'

By now the goose, satisfied that it had seen the intruder off, had retired to its domain, honking victoriously. That was one of many encounters with the feathered devils, and at dinnertime that day Gerard was regaled with an embroidered account of the confrontation.

We went back the following morning. Gerard led, with me following close behind and George keeping a cautious distance at the rear. We closed up when Gerard stopped to study the cottage and outhouses. Except for a boisterous rooster and his clucking hens, the homestead was a haven of sun-warmed peace. A butterfly zig-zagged across to land on the stone wall behind us.

Gerard turned to look reassuringly at us. 'There's nothing here to worry about. They must be locked up.'

Dead on cue an inharmonious honk answered him as a goose, its head and neck thrust forward like a walking stick, waddled from behind an outhouse, followed by two more. They stopped. Beady eyes fixed upon us, they began to weave in and out, the leader honking his orders as they prepared to charge.

'I don't like the look of this,' muttered George, peering over Gerard's shoulder.

The trio had the advantage of looking down on us from a slight slope.

'Those skitters are going to attack us,' insisted George.

'Ach, you worry too much,' said Gerard uneasily. 'They can't get over the wall.'

At that instant the geese decided to charge. We were momentarily stupefied as the three monsters bounced and bounded toward us until the realisation hit us that these were birds – they had wings, low stone walls were no deterrent to them. We scattered like chaff in the wind as the geese, honking wrathfully, cleared the wall. George's eyes were standing out like organ stops as, arms and legs flailing like windmills, he shot away in desperate flight. Gerard and I almost knocked ourselves out as, in our panic, we collided. I did not know which was worse, those huge flapping wings or the shrill cacophony from their protruding yellow beaks. We ran. My legs pounded the ground like pistons. Close behind me Gerard's boots scattered loose stones and his wheezing told me he was running out of steam. Racing past the open cottage door, I was vaguely aware of a figure armed with a raised broomstick issuing forth.

'Mother of God,' yelled the mistress of the cottage as she laid into the geese. 'Ye screeching divils! I'll wring yer scrawny necks! Away with ye.' Their feathers flying, she diverted our attackers into a corner and finally forced them, in complete disarray, back to their lair.

I was a wreck, barely able to draw breath, but the sight of Gerard, spreadeagled on the grass, his chest heaving and sweat pouring off him, beads of it glistening on top of his bald head, had me doubled up with laughter.

'I'm glad you think it's so funny,' he said, scowling at me. 'I don't.'

'Nothing to worry about, you said. They can't get over the wall, you said. Talk about famous last words,' I retorted.

'Jeeze,' Gerard went on, 'I never knew geese could shift so fast. It was only the thought of them pecking my arse that kept me ahead.'

At this point our rescuer arrived, concerned at the sight of us sprawled on the grass. She wanted to know if we were all right.

'Ach, we're OK, but those geese of yours scared the bloody life out of us. They're vicious,' Gerard told her.

'Aye,' she agreed, 'the conniving divils gang up on me poor wee dog. He's scared witless of them.'

'Giving him a dog's life,' quipped Gerard.

For the first time he had enough breath to laugh.

'If it wasn't for their eggs, I'd stretch their gangly necks.' Our neighbour pulled her headscarf tighter under her chin as she looked back along the path. 'Where's the other wee fella?' she asked. 'Mind ye, the way he was moving, a hare couldn't have caught him.'

Gerard and I cocked an eye at each other. We had been so caught up in the tribulations of the moment that we had forgotten George. Eventually, we came upon him further up the hill, propped up against a boulder. He was fuming, brows drawn, puffing furiously at his cigarette. He glared at us.

'A couple of real smart alecs, you two. Those gits were even worse than the one that chased me yesterday. I told you they were going to go for us.'

He was in a belligerent mood, indulging in bad-tempered argument with us until we, at last, cajoled him back to the cottage for a conciliatory Guinness. He had been badly frightened and perhaps Gerard and I should have been more sympathetic but we couldn't help laughing over the incident.

We never did solve the problem of the geese and they plagued us for the remainder of the holiday. Each of us, at some time or other, had to run or resort to cunning to escape their attentions. 'Did you see those bloody geese this morning?' became part of our daily conversation.

Just beyond the lair of the dreaded geese was a half-slated cottage. I got into the habit of chatting to the occupant about how the islanders grew things. He was always working on the lazy beds, used to grow potatoes. One day when he was complaining about the underlying rock I amazed him by telling him that my father could dig a few spadefuls of topsoil before he hit clay.

'Clay, is it? Well, just listen to this.' He banged his spade down beside the lazy bed and it clanged on solid rock less than half a spade deep. 'I wish to God I could lift a spadeful of soil just once,' he lamented. 'We have to scratch to build up a foot of it to grow the spuds. It's only the seaweed we drag ashore for fertiliser that allows us to grow anything. It's hard work. We take out the small stones with a crowbar and a sledgehammer and any cracks we fill in with the wee stones to stop the juices leaking away as the seaweed rots down.'

The seaweed, he explained, was gathered at low tide and packed into baskets and lashed each side of a donkey for transport to the fields. I spent many an hour watching him spread the seaweed. He was easy to draw because he took his time. Everything was done at a leisurely pace but it continued, nevertheless, until it was finished. This was no eight to five factory job. It went on till sunset if necessary but he always had time to light his pipe and have a bit of crack with this odd young fella from the black North, who did nothing all day but make marks on paper. Pádraig, as he was called, told me that the seaweed was sometimes dried on walls or placed on the beds to rot for several weeks. Lazy

beds were about four feet wide and as long as the available space allowed. The make-up of the bed consisted of whatever came to hand – seaweed, turf ash, decaying vegetables, animal dung. The dismantled thatch from a disused cottage, for instance, was a prize worth having. Setting the potatoes was a delicate business, Pádraig told me. They had to be put in deep enough to escape marauding birds but not too close to the decaying seaweed, which could burn them and prevent them from sprouting. Watching Pádraig's children pushing seaweed-laden wooden wheelbarrows reminded me of watching my father cutting his seed potatoes. He did not realise how lucky he was to be working the rich soil of County Antrim compared with the task of squeezing a living out of this rocky terrain.

I learnt a lot from Pádraig about working the lazy beds and I gradually became aware that he was very curious about life in the North. Whenever we

discussed island life the conversation somehow always returned to the war years, the blackout, the bombing of Belfast and the shipyards. He could not conceive of ships so huge that they needed thousands of men to build them.

I guessed that Pádraig had probably seen about fifty summers, but in that time he had only left the vicinity of Inishlacken and Roundstone once, to visit Galway. He had spent one night there and he had no intention of going back. He had never had a holiday and had no interest in visiting foreign places whether they were fifty or two hundred and fifty miles away. Being content, he claimed, was what mattered. There were a few material possessions he would have liked to have but as he had lived this long without them they were of no consequence.

'I've heard people say that at one time there were nearly two hundred people living on Inishlacken. There's not many left now, Pádraig,' I said. 'Do you think your children will settle for living here?'

He did not know. As for himself, he said that if the others left, he would go too. They were dependent on each other, especially in times of sickness or when harsh winter conditions cut them off from the mainland. I asked old Séamus and Michael the same question. They said they would stay so long as the others did, but both George and Gerard thought that the population had declined so much that it was on its last legs.

There were times when I felt quite guilty about distracting Pádraig from his work. However, it took little to persuade him to down tools, light his pipe and talk to me as long as I felt like listening. Life on the island had its own pace and discipline. Sometimes I would spend two hours or more with my back against a stone wall sketching while Pádraig toiled away.

One morning as Gerard, George and I sat sunning ourselves outside the cottage George said, 'Right, I'm off!' This was the code for announcing his morning ritual in the old schoolhouse.

'I wish he would go somewhere else for a change,' muttered Gerard. 'Have you been in there lately? He's made enough stone pyramids to build a wall.'

This reminded me of something which had puzzled me and I mentioned to Gerard the odd fact that I'd never seen an islander crouching behind a wall.

'They must have solved the problem better than us. After all, they've been here for generations.' He blew a smoke ring, flicking his ash aside. 'I've tried bringing up the subject to Michael in a roundabout sort of way, but either he didn't get my meaning or he didn't want to tell me.'

'Well, it has to be buried somewhere,' I said. 'I don't know how, though. You'd need dynamite to put a dent in this rock.'

Gerard kicked a loose stone, bouncing it down the path. 'I've a feeling it's a touchy subject. Short of asking a direct question, we'll never know.'

'I once read a book by Émile Zola called *Earth*,' I went on. 'This old crone grew the finest vegetables in the village, crisp and tender, marvellous taste. Guess what she used for manure?'

Gerard gave me a sideways glance. 'Yes,' he said, 'I've wondered about that too. Somewhere between the old thatch and the seaweed.'

Our pontifications were suddenly interrupted by angry yells emanating from the schoolhouse. George suddenly shot through the crumbling doorway with one hand hauling up his trousers and the other brushing at his face.

Gerard chuckled. 'He's been squatting over some nettles. I wonder where he got stung the most.'

George came charging up the path, scrubbing his face with a handful of grass. 'Any water in the bucket?' he shouted.

'Water won't help a sting. What's wrong?' asked Gerard.

'Bloody wind,' replied George. 'It blew the bum paper onto my face.'

Gerard and I looked at him in disbelief.

'You mean you've got crap on your face and you want to wash it off in our drinking water?' spluttered Gerard, jumping to his feet and blocking the door. 'No, you don't. Get you down to the beach and wash it there.'

I thought George was going to burst a blood vessel on the spot but he went charging off through the garden gate like a demented bull. Then Gerard and I collapsed on the bench, unable to move as we gave vent to our raucous laughter.

'In the name of God, did you ever see anything like that?' Gerard gasped, wiping the tears off his cheeks. 'How could anyone be so daft? How could he

get bumph stuck to his face like that?'

'He'll be back. If he's still talking to us, maybe we'll find out,' I answered.

Ten minutes later George reappeared, puffing vigorously at his cigarette, his brows drawn together and his little black moustache drooping even more than usual.

'C'mon, George, what the hell was that racket all about? You came up the path like you were running an Olympic sprint,' Gerard said to ease the tension.

George looked daggers at us for a second or so, then gave a sheepish grin. He shook his head. 'You'll never believe this,' he chuckled. 'I'd finished and I was bending down, looking for a stone to anchor the paper, when this bloody great whirlwind whipped the paper out of my hand. I looked up to see where it had gone and it landed smack right on my cheek.' George stared at the clouds racing across the sky. 'You know, this is the first breezy day there's been since we arrived,' he said. And then, as the thought struck him, 'All this chat about bogs reminds me — what are you going to do when Nano Reid arrives? You can't expect her to squat down behind a wall.'

Gerard shot bolt upright. 'Jesus, I never thought of that.'

'Well,' I said helpfully, 'now would be a good time to start.'

Inishlacken by George Campbell

'We could clear some of the turf out of the shed and put it in a bucket,' George suggested.

Gerard nodded his agreement.

'I've got a better idea,' I said. 'If we could get hold of an old oil drum, I could build a wooden frame around it. I've done it before when I stayed in the Mournes. There are tools and planking in the shed.' I was suddenly enthusiastic. I liked working with wood.

The idea appealed to Gerard. 'We could stack a lot of the turf outside and put the bog behind the door so that she can have a bit of privacy. We'll look around in Roundstone tomorrow for something.'

The whirlwind which had embarrassed George was the harbinger of a drastic change in the weather. By late that afternoon we found that we had to hold the pages of our sketchbooks down with clips, and watercolour washes that previously had been dry almost before the brush left the paper were now staying moist for ages. The sun was still shining but the wind had lowered the temperature and a dark bank of cloud was building up on the horizon. By teatime the weather took over the conversation as the wind got stronger and lines of white-capped breakers rolled in to pound against the beach.

When night fell the window frames were rattling as a gale howled over the island and we could hear, in quick succession, the crash and boom of the waves smashing over the harbour wall. Suzy Blue Hole hunched herself in one corner of the hearth, twitching her ears and staring at the door, uneasy at the rattling latch.

'If that wind doesn't settle soon there'll be too much sea running for us to go to Roundstone in the morning,' said Gerard, winding up his gramophone in an attempt to drown out the sound of the storm.

A tune emerged from the horn. George's feet began to tap and soon he was accompanying the music on his guitar. Before long Gerard and I were keeping time by slapping our hands against our legs and executing an impromptu jig. We fetched a few bottles of Guinness from the cupboard and fed the fire some turf, which burnt more and more fiercely as the wind increased in velocity. Shadows flickered over us and danced on the walls. It was all too much for Suzy Blue Hole. She slunk under Gerard's bed, her unblinking yellow eyes following us round the room. Bedsprings creaked as Gerard stretched himself out leaning toward the circle of light to read. I was crouched on a low chair, imagining pictures in the red glare of the turf.

George suddenly sat up. 'There's someone at the door,' he said.

I turned in surprise to look at Gerard. He was sitting up, staring at the door.

'I didn't hear anything. Did you, Jim?'

'No, but I was half-asleep, and the latch is rattling.'

Gerard leaned over to stare at the big alarm clock on the high mantelpiece. The hands showed a few minutes past eleven o'clock.

'It's very late for one of the islanders to call. Maybe it's Michael needing some help,' Gerard said without much conviction.

Through the windows there was nothing showing outside but a blackness darker than the pit. I hooded my hands against the windowpane to shut out the soft light of the lamp and the flickering reflections of the fire, and peered out. There was no one there. A prickle of unease raised the hairs on the back of my neck. Each of us stared at the coats bunched behind the door. The sleeve of one, caught on the latch, quivered as a wilder gust shook the door.

The screech of George's chair as it skated across the tiled floor almost scared me out of my skin. Slowly he walked to the door, holding it firm against the wind as he poked his head out. He stepped outside. We saw his dim shape passing the window. He had not latched the door properly behind him and a gust blew it open, raising a fog of turf dust. Gerard and I dashed to close it. George reappeared after a double circuit of the cottage, shaking his head in disbelief at finding nothing there. I could not get over the casual way he had dandered out. It would have taken a horse and cart to drag me out into that darkness. From the expression on Gerard's face I could see that he felt the same.

'I'm telling you, I heard knocks on that door. Three knocks. And don't tell me it was the wind. I know the difference between a knock and a rattle,' said George, speaking more to convince himself than us.

'You were nearer the door,' I said. 'Maybe the noise of the wind in the chimney stack drowned the sound of it for us.'

'Three separate knocks you heard?' Gerard asked. He looked uneasy.

George nodded. He stared at Gerard's strained face. 'You've heard them before?'

'At least once before. Last winter, in the middle of another howling gale, with the rain lashing down like stair rods.'

I kept forgetting. George and I were transients, visitors enjoying a summer in the sun. Gerard was a resident, this was his home for a year. He had already had part of one winter here and faced another.

'Yes,' he went on, 'they were unmistakable. Three knocks. I opened the door expecting to see one of the islanders soaked to the skin standing there. But there was nobody. I know I heard three knocks.'

I said that there must be a logical explanation. The knocks seemed to happen in a high wind – maybe they were loose slates slapping on a rafter. George insisted that there had been three knocks on the door and he had felt absolutely certain that there was someone out there. He had been flabbergasted when he found that there wasn't. This has got him rattled, I thought. Between the two of them they had got me rattled as well. And I hadn't heard anything. We sat gazing at the fire, at the little darts of flame dancing across the surface. Our early exuberance had vanished. I was reminded of an evening when I was a child and somebody had dared me to run through a graveyard in the dark. Nothing happened but it had scared the living daylights out of me.

When I finally retired for the night I found that I could not sleep and I lay buried in my blankets trying to read by candlelight with a flame that danced about in the draught from a warped window frame. A mumble of conversation filtered through the bedroom door. Eventually the sound of the wind whistling round the cottage and the rhythmic pounding of the sea lulled me to sleep. Gerard was quite shaken by the knocking incident, and unable to sleep, huddled in front of the fire until dawn.

The storm was still raging the following morning. The noise and the wan light told me that we would not be going to Roundstone that day. Perhaps, I thought, we ought to have gone the previous day. By nightfall Gerard and George would be chewing their fingernails for want of a cigarette. There wouldn't be a butt left to share between them. I was not a cigarette smoker and I still had half a pouch of Mick McQuaid tobacco. The whiff of the sweet-smelling aroma from my cherrywood would probably reduce the two of them to salivating wrecks. It was my turn to cook. Deciding what to feed them was always a problem but the storm simplified things. There was not much of anything to choose from.

I looked out of the window at the waves exploding over the harbour wall contrasting with the black clouds that clung tenaciously to the horizon. There seemed to be no sign of the storm abating. Gerard was still asleep, having crawled into his bed as the sky began to lighten, but George was showing signs of life as I poked through our remaining food supply. There was even less than I expected. The bread bin was only a quarter full but the spuds might last another two or three days.

'Would you look at that sea!' George said complainingly. 'We won't make it to Roundstone today.'

I pointed out the currach still lying on the grass; even the children hadn't been able to get to school. Later I went outside to do some pen and ink sketches instead of the usual watercolour. I left Gerard and George dithering about what to do. George loathed the wind. I suspected that he would just read a book or mooch around, irritating the hell out of Gerard and me as he usually did when he was forced into a situation that did not appeal to him. Being marooned by the weather on an island with a diminishing supply of cigarettes was likely to be one such situation.

'The way the weather is looking,' he said mournfully, 'we won't make it to Roundstone tomorrow either and by this evening we'll be out of fags.'

Gerard looked at him and said unfeelingly, 'Well, you'll just have to sit on your arse and make the best of it.'

When I returned to make the dinner I found Gerard working alone at his easel. He never liked working outdoors but he had an incredible memory for shapes and colours. Once he had worked out a picture in his mind, he could work it up on the easel in the cottage.

'He hates the wind,' Gerard said, glancing in the direction of the bedroom where George was reading. 'Mind you, he hates thunder and lightning even more. I've seen him under the table panic-stricken in a thunderstorm.'

'The weather's not that bad,' I said. 'I was able to find enough shelter to get some drawing done.'

By teatime George was beginning to get a bit fraught. He had moved our bench round to the gable end of the cottage to get some shelter and had spent the afternoon sitting on it, gazing in the direction of Roundstone – at a paradise full of cigarette shops and glasses of Guinness.

'It doesn't look any better than it did this morning,' he growled, munching his toast. 'That bloody wind is blowing harder than ever. And I haven't seen an islander all day.'

Gerard tried to persuade him to count his blessings. After all, he pointed out, we were on dry land with a roof over our heads and not tossing about like a cork on the waves.

However, George would not be cheered up. He took out his cigarette packet and extracted one. 'This is my last,' he announced, as though he had just been sentenced to be shot at dawn.

Gerard shrugged. 'Join the party. I've smoked my last one too.'

It was my usual custom to smoke my pipe after tea but this was one evening when I thought it prudent to leave my cherrywood on the mantelpiece.

'We can't just sit here all evening watching the fire,' I said. 'Anyone want to come for a wander round the island?'

George did not raise his eyes from his book. It was obvious that he had no intention of getting his head blown off watching the waves smashing onto the beach.

Taking our jackets from their pegs behind the door, Gerard and I set off. The wind tugged and battered us but it was not cold. Spray, blown high over the stone-walled path, had us running for cover at times as the wind battled with the waves. It flattened the scanty grass and played eerie tunes as it howled

through gaps in the walls and roofless cottages sheltering sheep and donkeys. Only the mountain tops were visible. Roundstone and the shoreline were hidden in the haze of spray.

'It's marvellous but I wouldn't stand here in the dark for a pension,' Gerard said soberly.

I turned my back on the wind to answer him. 'Why do you say that?'

'Those knocks on the door last night. George was absolutely sure that there was someone there. He had to walk round the cottage twice, and in that wind too, to make sure that there wasn't. Well, that was exactly my reaction when it happened to me last winter. I had the strongest feeling that someone was definitely there.' Gerard was obviously still uneasy about the incident.

'Gerard,' I said, 'I honestly didn't hear a thing but between the two of you and the knocks I never heard I was jittery enough to want to stick my head under the blanket. I can't explain why.'

'Well,' he said, 'try living here alone in the winter. I guarantee you'll be more than a little jittery.'

I did not doubt that he was right. We never heard the knocks again, but long afterwards Gerard would insist that there was something uncanny about them.

As night drew on the wind seemed to get stronger. We clustered together round the hearth as a fine film of turf dust filled the room. We did what we could to combat it by covering our bucket of drinking water with a newspaper and inverting the cups on the dresser.

In the absence of a wireless set our news, whether local or global, came from the newspaper we bought on our trips to Roundstone and I was reading an old copy of the *Irish Times* when an exasperated George put his book down.

'Christ, I'm dying for a smoke,' he moaned. 'This is killing me. If I see Michael I'm going to ask him if he's got any cigarettes to spare.'

Gerard looked at him over the top of his glasses. 'You can't do that. You can ask for help in an emergency but not for bloody cigarettes. These islanders are so self-sufficient that it's only in dire straits that they will ask for anything. So forget it, I have to live here after you've gone. I don't want the whole place buzzing about you going to pieces because you had to do without a smoke for a couple of days. And you had better realise that by the sound of the wind we won't be in Roundstone tomorrow either. Even if the wind dies down during the night, the sea will not be calm enough until teatime.'

An expression of incredulity registered on George's face. 'Are you telling me that it could be another two days before I can have a smoke?'

Before Gerard could continue I interrupted. 'It seems to me that we should be worrying more about grub than smokes. Today is Wednesday. I reckon that by Friday there won't be a crust left in the bread bin. We have just about enough spuds to give us dinner on Friday and that's it.'

'That is an emergency,' said Gerard. 'Let's hope we don't have to act on it. Folks in Roundstone will laugh their heads off. I'll bet you anything that right this minute they're wondering how we're coping.'

George was livid. 'We should have gone to Roundstone before the storm got up,' he cried. 'If we had, none of this would have happened.'

'You say that again and I'll bend that bloody saucepan over your skull. You are the greatest, girning wee skitter I ever came across.'

There was only one person in the land of the living who could speak to George like that and get away with it – Gerard. George swung sideways in his chair, his mouth slack in astonishment, black brows knitted, brown eyes flashing like buttons. His glare riveted Gerard to his chair. The silence stretched as taut as thread and then snapped when an attack of catarrh set George snorting and blowing great blasts into a large handkerchief which he hauled out of his pocket with the dexterity of a magician. He noisily blew his clogged nose, put his handkerchief back, and then returned to his book as though nothing had happened. I glanced sideways at Gerard. He raised his eyebrows. Both of us knew that if nature had not intervened, giving him time to cool off, Gerard would have been skewered by George's sarcasm.

The only sound was that of the wind howling round the cottage accompanied by the roar of the surf. The unaccustomed silence between us unnerved me.

'George,' I ventured, 'would you fancy a pipe of tobacco? It might settle your longing for a smoke.' I fetched my cherrywood, rammed a pipe cleaner up the stem and handed it over with my pouch of Mick McQuaid. 'Here, fill up and have a puff.'

He looked undecided. 'The last time I smoked a pipe the taste nearly killed me.' He gave the barrel a good sniff.

'Just smoke it. Don't inhale it or it will make you even more bad-tempered

than you are now,' Gerard said, grinning.

My heart sank. Surely Gerard wasn't going to goad him again.

'Just you keep quiet, I've had enough of your lip for one evening,' George answered, but without malice.

Laboriously, the pipe was filled. Clouds of smoke eddied round his head as he lit up, increasing with every puff until he looked like a headless body lost in a fog. Hanging on to the end of a pipe was an inappropriate image for George. The huge bowl of the cherrywood sticking from his gob and his little black moustache rising and falling with every puff gave him a comical appearance. We watched him smoking happily as he rocked his chair onto its back legs. Shortly afterwards he laid the pipe aside and returned to his book.

'Did you enjoy that?' I asked.

He nodded half-heartedly, saying it was all right but that he wasn't crazy about it. I went back to my newspaper while Gerard set about making some tea by dropping the kettle down a link on the chain that supported it above the fire. There was one packet of biscuits left in the tin. Gerard advised us to make the most of them.

I held up an article about the Queen's visit to Belfast and thus triggered off the second squall of the evening.

'It mentions her admiring John Luke's mural in the city hall. I climbed up the scaffolding while he was painting it to have a look and a chat before I left Belfast.' This was an experience I was not likely to forget as it was twenty feet off the ground.

'How does it look? I've never seen it,' Gerard said.

'It's a half-moon shape about thirty feet wide and fifteen feet at the highest point. It's very precise and well-executed, as you would expect from John. A bit too decorative for me, but I daresay the folk at the city hall will like it. You know, he worked twelve hours a day for months on it. And all through the winter he had to wear two pullovers, his jacket, his overcoat and his hat and still he was frozen. I kept telling him to ask the people at the city hall to provide some heating, but he wouldn't.'

'I wonder how much they paid him,' George mused. He was not an admirer of Luke's work.

Connemara Landscape
by George Campbell

'Five hundred pounds, he told me. Not much for all that work and the time it took, not to mention the arctic conditions. Someone told him, unofficially, that he might get another two hundred pounds.'

'That's bloody generous of them,' muttered Gerard. 'They should have given him double that amount.'

'John Hewitt gave it a good write-up in the paper,' I said. That was my mistake.

'He would,' growled George. 'He should stick to his poetry.'

George had never forgiven Hewitt for his critique on Ulster artists in which he had praised Luke and Colin Middleton but said that, in his opinion, Campbell, Dillon and Dan O'Neill had yet to fulfil their earlier promise. Consequently, he was barely tolerated by the offended trio. I felt obliged to defend Hewitt, who had encouraged me by buying sketches and small oils at a time when I was seriously impoverished.

'Well, whatever you do, don't let him influence you with his high-faluting theories.' George was determined to have the last word on the subject.

I yawned over my tea and biscuit. Although the weather had curtailed our activities it had, nevertheless, been a long day. I hoped for a softer day tomorrow.

Waking in the morning was one of the pleasures of living on Inishlacken. I would lie in bed listening to the island's first stirrings – the bleating of sheep against the distant boom of the surf, the screaming of seagulls, and later the laughter of children as they gathered on the harbour wall for the long row to Roundstone. Not on this day, however. I awoke to the sound of the wind wailing as relentlessly as ever. There was nothing peaceful or serene about this morning. Nor about my companions, either, when it penetrated their sleep-fogged heads that the weather was as inclement as ever. It was going to be a grumpy day. No smokes after breakfast, the bread turning stale, and the dreadful feeling of confinement caused by being unable to open the door as we usually did. I could see that Gerard was beginning to suffer from the want of a cigarette but I was also quite sure that not a word of complaint would he utter within earshot of George.

Incredibly, it had been only the wind that had tormented us. There hadn't been any rain. However, I decided that, high wind or not, I would go out that day to sketch. Gerard opted to work indoors on his oil. He was temperamentally more suited to island life than George, being blessed with patience. George was much more volatile; he was a fidget who needed to be constantly on the move, mentally as well as physically. He could exhaust himself by being able to maintain a high level of restlessness for hours on end. Today would be one of those days. I felt sorry for Gerard if they were to spend the whole day cooped up together.

I was barely a hundred yards from the cottage when I encountered Pádraig knocking a hole in a wall to let his sheep graze in an adjoining field.

'What about this wind, Pádraig?' I asked. 'When do you think it will drop enough to let us get to Roundstone?'

He straightened, and pushed his cap to the back of his head. 'Ach, we usually get a bit of a blow around the end of April or the beginning of May. It's late this year but it shouldn't last more than another couple of days.'

I told him that the lads would not be pleased to hear that. Come to think of it, I was not too happy about it myself. Our food supply had become dreary, stale and repetitive. I longed for a wedge of fresh cheese with a soft bap still smelling of the oven.

'How are you faring?' Pádraig asked.

'Not too badly,' I lied. 'The Guinness is running low but I daresay we'll manage.' If I had said anything else Gerard would have killed me.

Pádraig laughed. 'You can always sweeten it with a drop of *poitín*. It'll make it last longer and make you forget the blow.'

This was a chance that might never come again. Tales of *poitín* were rife and got more lurid the further a person was removed from the stuff. 'Lethal' was the adjective usually applied to the beverage.

'If we were looking, do you know where we might find a drop or two?' I asked.

A twinkle lit his eye. 'Aye, oh aye, I can get ye a mouthful or two of the finest home brew ye ever tasted. Just ye say the word.'

'Thanks, Pádraig, the lads will appreciate your offer. With the weather what it is, they could do with something to cheer them up.' Especially George, I added to myself.

We ambled back towards his cottage, seeking shelter from the everlasting wind. Pádraig's pipe glowed red as we huddled close to the wall of an outbuilding. The interior of the cottages fascinated me. I was longing to be asked inside to see what they looked like. All I had managed so far was a peek through an open door while I was waiting to collect some eggs. I really wanted to draw some interiors but I could not bring myself to trespass on the hospitality of the people by asking permission. However, as no such invitation seemed to be forthcoming, I decided to fall back on what Gerard called my native cunning.

'When I was drawing the outside of your cottage yesterday, I noticed that there's a wee window in the gable end. Is there a room up there?'

'Oh, that's just a loft to store bits and pieces. Can't waste good space. Mind ye, there's room enough for a bed,' answered Pádraig.

The windows in the low thick walls were so small (in order to keep out the weather) that the rooms were always dark unless the door was left open. I was hoping that Padraig would say, Come in and see for yourself. But he didn't, so I gave up.

'The only good thing about this weather is that it keeps those bloody geese penned in,' I said with feeling.

He burst out laughing. 'Aye, I heard all about that. The wife was doubled up laughing.'

I had to grin at the recollection.

'We didn't think it funny at the time but we had a good laugh about it afterwards. So you think there'll be no change in the weather?' I added with some resignation.

His eyes scanned the horizon before he shook his head. 'It'll be tomorrow or maybe the next day before it stops,' he answered.

I hunkered down behind a wall to get enough shelter to draw. The view would have warmed the heart of any painter. Despite the wind, it was not cold. Row upon row of white-capped breakers raced down on Inishlacken until they crashed on the rocks with an almighty roar. Marvellous.

When I arrived back at the cottage Gerard seemed to be in a very good humour.

'We had a visitor while you were out. It was old Séamus. He could hardly stand in the wind. We offered him a cup of tea but we had to explain that we had no smokes. He insisted on giving us three apiece.'

'You haven't smoked them already?' I asked, thinking George looked a lot happier.

'Well, we had to have one to keep the old fellow company,' said Gerard. 'I'm saving the rest for tonight. We've got beans, bacon, a few fried spuds and tea for dinner. We're hoarding what few biscuits are left for supper.'

It was a sparse meal but it took the edge off our hunger. The larder was now nearly empty; we had one tin of peas, less than half a packet of biscuits, enough butter, nine slices of dubious-looking bread, plenty of eggs and – we counted them – ten spuds.

Gerard slouched in his chair, Suzy Blue Hole at his feet, toasting her nose in front of the turf fire.

'If we can't get to Roundstone tomorrow, hunger will be gnawing at our bellies,' he observed.

'What do you mean, tomorrow?' I lamented. 'I'm bloody starving now and I've just had my dinner.'

'Jim complaining about being hungry – that's something we don't hear very often, eh, Gerard?'

'Ach, let him be, he's a growing lad,' replied Gerard.

George was biting his nails. 'Well, what do we do for grub when we've eaten the last scrap?'

'Let's worry about that tomorrow – this weather can't last that much longer. If it calms down we'll be in Roundstone before you can turn round.'

Gerard sounded very optimistic but I remembered what Pádraig had said and held my tongue.

We sat talking for a while and then Gerard said, 'Let's do each other's portraits. Come on, George, you've done nothing but sit on your arse for the last three days.'

In his way Gerard could be very persuasive and it was not long before George was taking out his pen and ink while he himself got out his watercolours. I was the first sitter. They were soon beavering away, heads down, glancing up now and then to scrutinise or make a comment on the shape of my ears or something.

George was the next sitter and, as usual, fidgeted all the way through it, completely unable to keep his head still.

'Hurry up,' he complained, 'my neck's going to be as stiff as a poker by the time you two are finished.'

When we were done, Gerard and I signed and dated our efforts and handed them to him. He seemed pleased and tucked them carefully amongst his own drawings. Then it was Gerard's turn to sit.

'Do you remember what happened to your last portrait?' I asked, glancing at his round shiny dome.

'I forget.'

'Naw, you don't. Langtry Lynas?'

'Jesus, I'd forgotten all about that.'

Langtry Lynas was a Belfast artist, old and small, with an artistic appreciation that began and ended with the Pre-Raphaelite Brotherhood. Nothing existed for him beyond those pillars of Victorian art. A year earlier we had mounted a group exhibition at 55A Donegall Place, which besides the three of us, had included Arthur Armstrong, Tom McCreanor, Dan O'Neill, Leslie Zukor and George's brother, Arthur Campbell. Shortly before the official opening Langtry Lynas shambled up the stairs, his stick clattering on every boarded step. We could tell it was him long before he burst through the tall glass door.

'It's that wee bollocks again,' hissed Dan O'Neill.

Langtry's usual custom was to stand in front of each painting, muttering and complaining about the hideous, degenerate art on display. Most of the time we ignored him, objecting only when he deterred

Man with Lamp by Gerard Dillon

potential buyers. On this occasion he had barely arrived when we heard a dreadful thwacking noise reverberating round the gallery. He was attacking Gerard's self-portrait – knocking the living daylights out of it with his stick. We stood, momentarily, dumbfounded, and then he moved on to the next painting, which was one of Dan O'Neill's. With an oath, Dan rushed at Langtry, grabbed him by his cape and swung him off the ground. However, in the ensuing fracas Dan came off worse when Langtry, still laying about him with the stick, caught him a whack between the legs, rendering him knock-kneed with pain. Langtry attempted to make a dash for the door, only to be collared by an enraged and pain-driven Dan who helped him on his way by bouncing him onto the landing and threatening to throw him down the stairs if he ever showed his nose in the gallery again. He never did.

Gerard laughed as he recalled the incident. 'The bloody wee sod ruined a perfectly good frame. Did I ever tell you the outcome? Well, the painting was eventually bought by this guy who complained about the damaged frame. When I explained what had happened he asked me to put the story in writing, sign it and paste it on the back of the picture.'

George howled with laughter, saying that he probably hoped the note would double the picture's value over the next twenty years.

Later, when Gerard and I went out for a much-needed breath of the salt-laden air, the light overhead was blushing violet-grey. We left George behind, lost in his novel. He was not interested in our nocturnal meanderings. His idea of a spot of fresh air was a leisurely stroll in the warm sunshine. Dodging clouds of spray and battling with the elements was not his cup of tea. I swayed in the wind with my eyes narrowed, searching the wide sweep of the Atlantic for any sign of a break in the cloud that had blighted our lives for the past few days.

'Look over there, Gerard, at the colour of the horizon. That looks like the beginning of a change.' I was ever the optimist.

The wind snatched away his answer but he nodded his head. I also pointed out that the grasses were lying at a different angle. I knew because I had been buried in them for the previous three days. Our mood lightened immediately. A shift in the wind direction must mean a change in the weather at last. It had to be for the better.

After a while we returned to the cottage. Six black jars of Guinness remained. We sank them slowly so as to appreciate the bitter taste. Tomorrow, we told each other, Guinness from a barrel would taste even better. Booze was all very well, I thought to myself, but given the choice, I would opt for a bap crammed with fresh cheese. I dozed off dreaming of a table stacked high with goodies.

Next morning when I awoke I lay listening for the wind. The scream of the gale had gone and sunlight painted patterns on the floor. My companions were still snoring as I ate my solitary, meagre breakfast. The last one on short rations, I hoped, as I gazed out of the window. The turbulent rollers of yesterday were reduced to half their size, although they still looked daunting enough to block our passage out of the harbour.

I went out quietly into the clean morning air. The dark, threatening cloud had gone and the sea sparkled with a million diamonds, clear to the horizon. Already the sun was casting deep purple shadows behind walls and rocks and the harebells were lifting their heads again with only a quiver of their stems to acknowledge a passing breeze.

An island child stood by a bollard looking out to sea.

'Hello, Patrick. Are you longing to get back to school?'

His flaxen mop hung round his steel-rimmed glasses. There was an impish air about him. 'I'm looking to see what the blow brought in,' he answered, peering along the rocks beyond the harbour wall.

I leaned over. All I could see were pieces of timber stranded on the beach. I asked him if he ever found anything good. Patrick told me that last year he had found a drum of oil, a life buoy and a big rope inside a wooden box. I asked him if he looked every time there was a storm.

'Aye, we all have a look.'

'When do you go back to school?'

'Monday.'

'You didn't expect to get a week's holiday in June, did you?'

He shook his head.

'Do you get many holidays in the winter?' I asked.

He nodded vigorously. 'Sometimes when the weather is bad we get two weeks. Once we had three weeks off,' he said gleefully.

Patrick, one of the island children

I was appalled at the idea of being cut off for three weeks. The last few days were just a hiccup compared to that.

'What about your lessons when you're cut off?'

'Teacher always tells us to do sums and to write things.'

'And do you?'

'Me ma makes me.'

We both laughed at that. Some things are the same north and south of the border. I asked him what he had done all week when he wasn't at school. He told me that he and his ma and da and the donkey had been gathering weed and stacking it up behind the wall.

'Did the blow bring much of it in?'

'Oh aye, it was all over the place.'

'You worked hard, then?'

He gave me a shy grin but said nothing.

'Come on then, I'll walk back with you and see if I can do a bit of beachcombing.'

I walked right round the island but I found no treasure.

Apart from old Séamus and Pádraig, we had not clapped eyes on anyone since Monday. I was short of more than food. I felt like a good natter. I needed someone else's brain to pick because there were so many things about life on the island that could not be explained except by tactful enquiries. For instance, while sheltering from the wind as I was sketching I picked up a beautifully marked stone lying close to the foundations of a wall. In the hollowed space beneath it lay two candles tied with rotting string. They looked as though they had been placed there deliberately. Why?

I was famished. Breakfast had barely taken the edge off my appetite and all I had to look forward to was a spartan dinner of three spuds and a fried egg. Not much to tempt me back to the cottage, but although I lingered along the way, not a single islander appeared. The ferocious wind had dropped to a light breeze and changed direction. With a bit of luck we would be in Connolly's bar this evening and with full bellies to cushion the impact of the Guinness.

When I returned to the cottage Gerard's oil was sitting on the easel, drying, and I was very impressed with it.

Gerard, however, dampened my enthusiasm. 'It's all right,' he said. 'I like it at the minute but I could well change my mind tomorrow.'

'It's a great composition,' I said. 'I can't work out how you managed to pull everything together.'

Gerard had an unerring sense of how to place an image on canvas and how to exploit the tension between shapes. He knew the potential of a rhythmical unbroken outline and he could use a single spot of bright colour to telling effect. Both George and he had explained to me the principle of positive and negative shapes but being told something and then being able to do it myself was something different. I sat in front of the painting for a time, oblivious to the presence of the other two while I worked out how the various shapes held the whole thing together.

'The spuds should be ready soon,' said Gerard, giving me a nudge as he probed the vegetables with a fork.

'I've been starving for the last three days,' I said. 'If my ma knew how I'm suffering, she'd have a parcel of sodas in the post for me.'

Gerard laughed. He peered out of the window. 'The sea has calmed a lot since this morning. I reckon we'll be able to make it across before teatime.'

As I watched the pot lid splutter as the water boiled over the spuds, I informed him that the first place I was going to was Connolly's for a jar and a feed of sandwiches.

'Where's George?' I asked.

'He went for a walk a while ago,' Gerard answered, 'About time too. The way he's been sitting around the house lately, I think rigor mortis was about to set in.'

George eventually reappeared looking considerably more cheerful than of late and announced that the wind had died away and that we would be able to go to Roundstone that afternoon. He looked determinedly at us, challenging us to disagree with him. For once we did not.

As Gerard laid the plates on the table I offered to drain the spuds. I carefully lifted the lid from the pot and started to empty the boiling water into a basin by the fire. Then disaster struck. The pot lid suddenly slid from my grasp, spewing boiling water and potatoes into the centre of the fire. A huge cloud of steam billowed up and the fire died. I could not speak as I crouched over the ashes. We were motionless with shock as we looked at our last precious meal scattered in the muddy turf. Water trickled in little rivulets across the hot, tiled hearth, bubbling in the little crevices. The turf had collapsed into a pathetic heap, with a single plume of acrid smoke marking the demise of our precious fire which had burnt continuously night and day.

Then all hell broke loose. George went spare, marching up and down, holding his head in both hands, swearing blue murder and threatening to kick my arse all round the island.

'MacIntyre, you bloody big troglodyte of an eejit, you've ruined our dinner! Christ, I was really looking forward to those spuds. That walk gave me an appetite. Oh God, I could hang the bugger!'

Gerard just shook his head. I was lost for words, embarrassed, and too miserable to do anything but stare at the havoc I had created.

George marched up and down. 'Jesus, no fags, incarcerated for the last three days and now, no grub. You realise, MacIntyre that we've eaten less than a bloody hen these last few days – and now this.'

I was convinced that he was going to beat my pan in.

Gerard was every bit as hungry and annoyed but he managed to avoid overreacting. 'C'mon, George, settle down. It was an accident. He didn't do it on purpose.'

I felt so bad that I lost my appetite. Gerard helped me to clean up the mess. We swept out the hearth and piled up sticks to relight the fire.

'Don't worry, it could have been worse. You might have scalded yourself,' he told me.

The turf was difficult to relight but finally it caught, sending a bright flame dancing up the chimney again. Gerard lowered the kettle onto the fire and we sat around patiently, waiting for it to come to the boil. The bench outside groaned as Gerard and I lowered ourselves each side of George. I took a cautious peek at him but he did not acknowledge our arrival.

'George, are you asleep?' Gerard poked him with his elbow.

He opened one eye and then shut it again. 'Keep that bugger away from me. I'm not talking to him.'

Gerard started to laugh. 'God, you should have gone on the stage. You missed your vocation. That was some show of bad temper. If that is typical, it's a wonder Madge hasn't dented your head with a saucepan before now.'

'Fart off!'

Half an hour later a steaming kettle provided us with a much-appreciated cup of tea. We drank it sitting in the sun, eyeing the ocean and calculating how long we had to wait before we dared launch the dinghy. Four o'clock announced itself on the clock.

'Right, get the gear. We're going,' Gerard said.

We did not need telling twice. Grabbing empty shopping bags, we sprinted for the beach to launch the boat. The sea was still very choppy, much worse than anything we had experienced before. We bounced over the waves, slid down into troughs, throwing spray across the stern and into our eyes. We brushed it away, hardly noticing it in our eagerness to get to Roundstone.

4

We had barely reached the outskirts of the town when we met one of Gerard's many friends.

'Ah, it's yourself, Gerard. Are ye all right? I couldn't help wondering about ye and your friends. We were talking about ye last evening.' She seemed concerned.

'Things weren't too bad. The grub was running a bit low but here we are,' Gerard answered cheerfully.

A doleful expression flitted over his friend's face. 'It's a terrible affliction not being able to get off the island. God help the children missing so many lessons.'

'I don't think it worries them much,' said Gerard. He was eyeing George, who had kept on walking, with obviously no intention of lingering for a friendly chat. 'I have to go. We must get to the post office before it closes,' Gerard said apologetically. He gently touched her arm. 'I'll call later.'

Roundstone slumbered under the late afternoon sun. A shirt-sleeved man, his duncher low over one eye, prodded an obstinate cow along one side of the main street. There was no one else. Not a single boat was afloat in the harbour. The sun seemed to have soaked the vitality out of the place. Even the screams of the circling seagulls did nothing to disturb the somnolence. We had agreed on our priorities: cigarettes, the post office, groceries and Connolly's. The shopkeeper, however, had to hear all about our tribulations during the storm and the post office was on the point of closing when Gerard finally rushed in to see if there was any mail for us. He emerged with a clutch of letters, most of them for himself, one for George from Madge, and one for me.

The sight of Ma's sloping backhand writing immediately set me worrying about what might have happened to make her write to me, but she was just giving me hell for not letting her know I'd arrived. George was standing in the middle of the pavement reading his letter from Madge enquiring about his health and wellbeing. She wanted to know when he'd be back in Dublin.

'I'd have been back long ago,' he groused, 'if I'd known what my guts were about to suffer for three days and if I'd known that some eejit was going to throw my dinner on the fire.'

'When she hears what you've had to endure she'll never let you go away by yourself again.' Gerard dug him in the ribs.

George stuffed his letter in his pocket and went striding up the road towards the long-awaited pint, with Gerard and I not far behind.

Connolly's was deserted except for two old men who sat with their heads locked together, deep in conversation. As we walked in Carmel shouted to us that they'd been talking about us the previous night, wondering how we were getting on in the storm. Gerard did not have to enunciate the words; the look he turned on us said clearly, 'What did I tell you?'

Three pints of Guinness washed down three thick cheese sandwiches in a twinkling and a repeat order was called for.

'Are yous lads hungry?'

'Well, a wee bit. The sea air gives you an appetite. Isn't that right, boys?' Gerard looked at us for confirmation and we nodded as we downed the sandwiches and Guinness like there was no bottom to our stomachs.

Three rounds later, with our bellies full and our heads buzzing, we felt at peace with the world again. Gerard was at the bar, leaning across the counter, bending Carmel's ear. She glanced over at George, clapped her hands over her cheeks and screamed with laughter.

'I don't believe ye,' she shrieked.

'What is he telling her?' George asked, skewing round on his stool as she went into another paroxysm of laughter.

We heard Gerard say solemnly, 'God's truth.' He came back to our table with a smile winding up his moustache. 'I was telling her about the flying bum paper. It tickled her fancy.'

'Christ, it will be all over the town by this evening,' muttered George. 'Oh well, what odds? It'll give them a laugh.' He sank the rest of his Guinness in one gulp.

Suddenly, it seemed to me, the bar was filled with clouds of tobacco smoke and raucous banter. Sandwiches and Guinness hung like a dead weight in my stomach and I felt an overwhelming need for fresh air. I decided to go for a walk around the harbour.

As I wandered along, I remembered the impending visit of Nano Reid and our need of an old oil drum to improve our toilet facilities. It occurred to me that I might find one among the bushes alongside the harbour where the fishing boats dumped their rubbish. It was a good time to look, as the tide was out and I had room to poke about amongst the discarded rope, broken lobster pots, old paint tins and other junk. Eventually I found what I needed. It was a bit oily but handfuls of sand and thick wads of grass soon cleaned it up enough to handle.

I left it where we could pick it up on the way home and got back to the pub just as Gerard and George, their faces wreathed in boozy smiles, emerged carrying a sack filled with bottles of Guinness. Loaded down with bags of groceries, the Guinness and an empty oil drum, we looked like homeward-bound rag-and-bone men.

On the way back to the beach and the dinghy we passed a tinker's caravan. A shawled woman was attempting to light a fire with one hand while holding a baby in her other arm. She was having problems. Close by, two other children watched us with huge blue eyes. They were barefooted and in need of a good

scrub from head to toe. There was no man about.

George put down his load and walked over to squat beside the makeshift hearth. 'Here, let me do that for you.' He struck a match and blew on the twigs laid on top of the ashes. It must have been the Guinness on his breath, for in an instant flames were leaping upwards to lick the pile of dry wood, and the fire was started.

The woman thanked him profusely as she set a blackened teapot on top of the fire. She looked worn and tired, although she was not old, and her long dirty fair hair straggled over her shoulders. The infant, tightly wrapped in a shawl, slept soundly. The smallest children followed George as we moved off again. George's hand went into his pocket and came out holding two shining coins. Half-crowns – five shillings – a lot of money then. George was many things, but he could never be accused of meanness. I had seen him make similar gestures many times. He might have had a short fuse but he was generous with his time, his advice, and with his money – when he had any.

As we trudged on toward the beach, George suddenly commented that we must be daft not to have rowed direct to Roundstone instead of having to cart all the stuff miles to the boat. Gerard quickly reminded him that he hadn't been able to get across the water fast enough on the way out and that was why we'd taken the shortest route. It was a relaxed boatload of passengers that I rowed back to Inishlacken. The tribulations of the past few days were over and the sea had returned to its former gentle swell, giving us a quick crossing. The Guinness we had imbibed had given us an appetite and the smell of sausages, bacon, eggs and frying bread nearly drove me mad as we waited for them to cook. That evening we sat quietly around the turf fire, sampling the bottles of

Guinness we had brought back just to make sure they had not suffered from the sea journey.

Next morning I set about transforming the oil drum into our private convenience. A cerulean sky reached from the horizon and there was hardly a puff of wind to disperse the smoke from our chimney as it eddied upwards through the heat haze. A dog barked somewhere and dew sparkled on my boots as I made my way to the turf shed to look for enough scrap to build our loo. The saw I found had seen better days and its teeth needed sharpening, but it was good enough to split boards and angle corners and I soon had a neat square to fit snugly over the cylindrical drum. I fitted two rusty hinges to the wooden square for the lid, added a coat of white paint, with the lid picked out in blue to match our front door – and the job was done. I had slogged hard all morning and I was pleased with my efforts.

I called to the other two to come and admire the most luxurious bog that had ever graced the island. I pointed out to George that he could take his book to the bog and enjoy the peace and quiet. No more whirlwinds to disturb his concentration.

George was full of enthusiasm but Gerard warned him to wait until the paint had dried on the seat. There was still work to be done and we humped a small mountain of turf from inside the shed to a place beside the back wall to make room for Inishlacken's latest aid to personal hygiene. The closed door with the bog tucked in behind it gave a modicum of privacy and we were certain it would be much appreciated by Nano.

We had another problem in an ever-growing mountain of used tin cans. We burnt most of our rubbish but the cans were accumulating inside the old schoolhouse at an alarming rate. Anywhere else we could have disposed of them by digging a hole and burying them, but not on Inishlacken. However, my ingenuity knew no bounds. For an hour I worked away at flattening the cans between two big stones. The silence and serenity of the island was shattered by the sound of my banging as it echoed round the bare walls of the schoolhouse, eventually bringing George and Gerard out to investigate. They looked at the can mountain already reduced by half and I explained my plan of flattening the cans, putting them in a sack and dumping them in the sea

some two hundred yards offshore.

'You know,' said George, 'appearances can be deceptive. That lad has brains and sometimes he uses them.'

They were so impressed that I persuaded them to give me a hand with the rest. Later Gerard cooked a sumptuous dinner which left us bloated and lethargic as we sat on the bench in the sun, idly watching two islanders tethering the legs of half a dozen sheep before dumping them in a currach. We tracked their progress towards Roundstone until we finally lost them, tiny dots in a blue-green sea.

About half an hour later Gerard suggested a swim. He and I had been swimming on several occasions and had enjoyed plunging into the breakers before they pounded the beach. Fifteen minutes was usually enough. The Atlantic off the west coast of Ireland is not famous for its warmth. George hated water. We had tried to coax him in, time and again, but without success.

'Come on, George,' cajoled Gerard, 'get your toes wet just this once. You don't have to dive in. I promise you, once you are in you'll love it and you can tell Madge that you've swum in the Atlantic.'

George did not budge an inch.

'How have you managed to live all these years without taking a dip? I don't know how you can admit that no water has touched your brow since you were baptised.'

George ignored him.

Gerard and I had been splashing about in the breakers for some time when Gerard suddenly shouted, 'Christ, would you look at that!'

We stood waist deep in the water and watched as George, dressed only in baggy underpants, apprehensively dipped a tentative foot in the sea.

'Come on, it's not going to bite you. Get out a bit further and turn your back on one of those breakers,' yelled Gerard.

George presented a comical sight, with his white skin and those baggy shorts clinging to his vital parts like wet paper. He waded further out and then went at it with gusto, jumping up and down in the foam and shouting that his brass knobs were dropping off with the cold. To give him his due he was being very plucky, considering his dislike of the sea. After a short time he roared that he had had enough and was coming out.

Gerard and I did not hear him properly, as we were just surfacing after being submerged by a big wave. As we gasped and brushed the water from our eyes Gerard cried, 'Suffering Jesus, what's the man doing?'

I turned quickly, in time to see an arm and a leg waving above the foam. George was upside down in four feet of water.

'Get him out quick,' Gerard shouted.

We were fifty feet away and hampered by the waves rolling in. We tried to swim to him. Suddenly his head broke water, spouting like a whale, as he struggled to suck some air into his lungs. We eventually reached him and each grabbed a flailing arm and hauled him toward the beach, trying to keep his head out of the water as we did so. His chest was wracked by wheezes, coughs and splutters as he fought for breath.

'Are you all right, George?'

George had hardly the strength to do more than nod his head.

'How the hell did you manage to get upended?' Gerard asked.

'I banged my toe on a bloody rock and I lifted my foot to see if it was broken. I was in agony. Next thing I was bowled over and my head was under. God, I thought I was drowning.' He groaned as he examined a bright red bruise on his big toe.

Gerard shook his head. 'Well, you managed to scare the hell out of us two. My heart is still beating at twice its normal rate. Don't go so far out next time.'

'What the hell do you mean, next time?' George came up to the boil fast. 'There's never going to be a next time. That was the last one.'

'My God, what's Madge going to say when she hears that when we finally got him into the sea, he was so cross he nearly drowned?' I asked, grinning.

'Keep quiet, you,' snapped George with a sour face. He was soon on his feet, a bit white round the gills, but seemingly none the worse for his ordeal.

Now that the drama was over, all three of us suddenly broke out in goose pimples and we beat a hasty retreat over the rocks towards the cottage.

'This little tale will do the rounds of his Dublin cronies as soon as he gets home,' Gerard whispered later as we sat drinking mugs of hot tea.

After a time I got restless just sitting around and decided to go off for a look at the deserted cottages. I enjoyed exploring them, reconstructing the rooms and imagining the lives of the families who once lived there. I had sketched floor plans and made notes on the building methods used for the walls, chimneys and doors. Using my boot as a rough measuring tool, I had paced out complete plans of cottages and outhouses. I was surprised to find most of the measurements were fairly constant over the whole island.

I was inside one of the cottages when a collie dog poked its black and white head round the bleached wooden frame of the old doorway. It was Patch, Pádraig's dog. I scratched his mane and got a battering from his tail. I thought he was on his own until loose stones clattered as footsteps crunched over pebbles just beyond the gable wall.

'You're not still drawing at this time of the evening, surely?' Pádraig's voice carried softly in the still air.

'No, not this time, Pádraig. We've had other things on our minds today so I've given it a rest.' I told him about George's ducking in the Atlantic and his avowal that he would never go into the water again.

'God's truth, he's a lucky lad. I hate the water meself. Niver go near it. Not since me brother was drowned when we were youngsters. I niver forgot it. Niver learnt the swimming. Come to that, few of us here can swim.'

'You mean none of the island's fishermen can swim?' I asked in amazement.

'Aye, that's right.' He nodded his head.

'Surely if you work the sea it would be wise for you to know how to swim?

After all, one slip could cost you your life.'

'Ach, that would only make ye a careless fisherman and ye'd take chances with yerself and the currach,' he replied, gazing over the Atlantic toward the distant horizon.

I changed the subject. I asked Pádraig what the wooden pegs sticking out of the wall were used for and was told they were probably for lamps or a picture. Then I told him about finding the candles tied with string in a hole in the foundations and asked him of their origins. They were put there for good luck, he told me; sometimes it would be a horseshoe or clay from holy places. I told him some of our good luck practices, such as the hanging of horseshoes on doors and putting coins and old newspapers in the foundations of buildings. His pipe was going well now and his halo of strongly scented smoke made me long for my own cherrywood. We walked together along the sea path. I enquired apprehensively as to the whereabouts of the geese.

He laughed. 'Giving ye a rough time, them geese, eh? There's no sign of them that I noticed.'

It was quiet in the cottage when I got back. George and Gerard were reading, each with a glass of Guinness within easy reach. As I pulled up a chair by the hearth, George laid down his book, stretched his arms towards the ceiling, indulged in an elaborate yawn and then announced, 'I think I had better go home next weekend. Madge says a couple of people were enquiring about buying paintings. I think she may be a bit fed up being on her own. You two don't have women to worry about you so you can please yourselves.'

'Don't give me that crap,' laughed Gerard. 'Since when have you ever done a single thing you didn't want to do?'

George's little moustache drooped and he shrugged his shoulders.

Gerard kept at him. 'Why don't you just admit it? You're dying to get back to your home comforts.'

'Aw, come on, just because I nearly fainted from hunger and then you two tried to drown me doesn't mean I'm fed up,' he said defensively. 'By next weekend I'll have been here for a month. That's not a short stint.'

'Oh well, there's most of this week left and all of next so there's plenty of time for you to enjoy yourself in safety.' Gerard was poking fun.

George suggested that we had a farewell party for him. This was very well received as a good way to say thank you to the islanders. Gerard suggested getting a fiddler in and having a *céilí*. George, a great lover of parties, began to calculate the number of journeys that would be required to the mainland to transport sufficient Guinness. I joined in, telling them of Pádraig's offer of *poitín*. I began to regret it as George turned a suspicious eye upon me.

'And when did he tell you that?'

'The other day.'

'You mean when our booze ran out?'

'Ah, well . . .'

George started to come to the boil again. 'You big bollocks, we could have done with some of the stuff there and then.'

Gerard was quick to intervene. 'That's over and done with. Tell Pádraig he and everyone else is invited to a party. Ask him to get us a bottle of mountain dew.'

As we talked a quiet tap on the windowpane heralded the arrival of Michael, his pipe jammed in one corner of his mouth and his hands buried deep in his trouser pockets.

'Well, lads, taking it easy, I see,' he said, pulling up a chair.

'The very man we want to see,' said Gerard. 'George is going home next weekend and we're thinking of having a wee farewell party for him. Will you pass the word that everyone's invited.'

Michael replied with a twinkle in his eye that George had only just arrived. 'It's a long time since we've had a party on the island,' he continued. 'The boys will be here to a man. Somebody will probably have to cart auld Séamus home. He's hardly fit to move these days and a few jars loosens both his tongue and his legs.'

We went on yarning and sinking jars of Guinness until it was dark enough to need the yellow light of our oil lamp to help out the firelight. It was pitch dark when Michael finally wiped his hands across his lips and set his glass down by the hearth. He stood, drawing up his pullover to tighten the *crois* round his trousers.

'That's a real colourful *crois*, Michael,' I remarked.

Michael nodded and smiled.

As the three of us rose to our feet to accompany Michael on part of his

Michael Woods

journey home, I happened to glance at Gerard and saw that he was rolling his eyes toward the ceiling. I was puzzled for a moment and then enlightenment struck. The *crois!* I suddenly realised that I had very nearly committed another faux pas.

A *crois* is a long woven woollen strip, usually about three inches wide and six to eight feet long. It has tiny bright splashes of colour woven through its length and has a fringe at each end. Men wind it around their waists to keep up their trousers. The best examples come from the Aran Islands. A few years earlier Gerard had returned to Belfast from a visit to the West, bringing with him a *crois*. George was captivated with it and was green with envy. He plagued the life out of Gerard to get him one. At parties he had Gerard hoisting up his pullover so that all and sundry could view this woven masterpiece of native art. George could not leave it alone: Gerard had to get him one and every time they met he would enquire if Gerard had managed it yet.

Finally Gerard's patience cracked and he promised to find one for him on condition that George did not mention the subject for two weeks. Two weeks of peace. George clamped his tongue. Gerard kept his word. Two weeks later George got a *crois* that was even more colourful than Gerard's original. George was ecstatic. Wherever he went he wore his *crois* and told the story of how Gerard had sent to the Aran Islands for it. It was his party piece. At the slightest sign of interest his jersey was yanked up and the *crois* was displayed. His trousers were always at the point of falling down as he unwound the *crois* to be admired.

For weeks Gerard listened patiently to George sounding off about this bloody marvellous *crois* all the way from the wild west of Ireland. Then one day he walked into Campbell's café in Donegall Square in Belfast to find George with a captive audience going on about his *crois*. Gerard was exasperated.

'Come on you over here,' he said, propelling George to one side. 'I'll tell you the truth about that bloody *crois*; it's never been near the Aran Islands. I made it on the back of a chair at home.'

George's mouth dropped open. For once he was speechless. Then he flew down the stairs, fit to be tied, yelling wrathfully that Gerard had had the nerve to charge him a quid for it. They fell out for a week until George came to his senses and started wearing braces again.

So *crois*es were a delicate subject and I had come close to resurrecting the affair. Luckily, however, George was distracted by Michael's departure and the arrangements for the coming party and the moment passed. This incident reminded me that Gerard was no slouch with a needle. He once took apart an old suit seam by seam and used the pieces as a pattern to cut out another suit from a length of tweed. When he appeared wearing it, no one would believe that he had tailored it himself. He also produced a few beautifully worked tapestries in his time and one of these was purchased by the Irish Tourist Board.

We parted company with Michael on the island path and watched as he continued on his way, his silhouette barely visible against the walls and massive boulders. We retraced our steps homeward by the light of a crescent moon which cast a shimmer across the harbour wall. Millions of stars studded the velvet dome overhead and the beautiful silent night enfolded us with only the distant lights of Roundstone to show where life was.

'You know, a night like this makes you forget all the trouble you have ever known . . .' said Gerard wistfully, ' . . . for a while.'

5

Next morning I listened to the familiar island sounds filtering through the open window. Suzy Blue Hole's silhouette on the curtains told me she was waiting for me to push the window open wider. As I parted the curtains she greeted me by purring and rubbing her head against the frame. I tickled her ears and looked out. It was going to be another scorcher.

George decided it was time to try the new construction. Twenty minutes later Gerard was speculating as to whether or not George had got stuck. I said he was probably just enjoying the peace. A minute later in walked George extolling the virtues of reading a newspaper in comfort on the bog.

We decided to go on a visit to Roundstone that afternoon to pick up some booze, food and odds and ends.

'When we go I want to ask exactly where Bulmer Hobson lives,' I said. 'I must pay him a visit soon.'

'You've been saying that since we arrived,' muttered George.

I was walking across to the far side of the island later on and came upon Pádraig herding two cows along the path. I asked him if he had ever heard of a man called Bulmer Hobson in Roundstone and if he knew anything about him.

Pádraig pulled his duncher low over his eyes. 'He was a great man for the politics,' he volunteered.

'Politics?'

'Ask him about it. He'll tell ye all ye want to know.'

He wandered off with his cows, leaving me sorely perplexed. Then I remembered the party and the *poitín* and I ran after him, invited him to the party, and conveyed Gerard's message about getting a drop. Pádraig said he would surely get some and that he'd be very glad to come to the party.

After dinner I told the others what Pádraig had said about Bulmer Hobson and politics. 'The only politician that I ever heard of down here is de Valera,' I went on. 'So Bulmer Hobson writes books and dabbles in politics about which nobody cares to comment.'

Gerard and George admitted that the name meant nothing to them.

We trooped down to the harbour and decided to head straight for Roundstone harbour to avoid more complaints from George. It was the long way and Gerard decided that it would be easier and quicker if he and I both rowed.

George took his seat in the stern, issuing orders like he was Captain Bligh adrift in the South Seas. 'You're off course, move over a bit to your left' – he was full of nautical terminology.

'What I want to know is why we're rowing our guts out while he sits there like Lord Muck shouting orders at us?' Gerard grunted as he heaved at the oars.

Halfway across I pointed to a large fish swimming lazily in circles far beneath us. The water was so clear that it was not hard to see. We rested on our oars to look at it but none of us had the least idea what kind of fish it was. George observed that it would have fed us for a week, as he hung over the stern watching it glide away. We were silent for a while as we picked up the rhythm and got the boat going again. It seemed extraordinary to be on an island surrounded by fish and not to have caught one. I hadn't fished since I was a kid and decided I might give it a try. I would get some line and hooks in Roundstone.

Our last visit to the harbour had left us looking like idiots. We had grounded the dinghy at half-tide and when we returned to it a few hours later it was well out of our reach in several feet of water. We had endured a lot of good-natured banter from the locals while they launched a currach to pull the dinghy back to the harbour steps. This time we were more careful and hauled it well out of harm's way.

The post office was our first port of call. I posted a card to Ma, assuring her that I was still in one piece and telling her that she could expect me back home around the end of June. There was a letter for Gerard. In the doorway we bumped into the parish priest. With a broad smile he enquired politely after our health as George and I squeezed past saying our good afternoons. However, he had poor Gerard pinned against the wall, squirming. We callously made our way to Connolly's, leaving him to his fate.

A few minutes later Gerard walked in with a face as long as a wet week. He had promised to go to mass on Sunday morning; he had run out of excuses, there was no alternative. Resting her arms on the bar, Carmel gave him a

Pub Scene
by George Campbell

welcoming smile as she handed him a letter that had been left for him. It was from Kate O'Brien, inviting us for supper on the following night.

'Oh, supper, indeed. Well, you two had better not give me the run-around you gave me last time or you can bloody well row yourselves home. So go easy on the Power's Gold Label,' I snorted.

Gerard took a large gulp of Guinness, wiping the froth from his moustache, before opening his letter from Belfast. 'It's from my mate Brendan Madden,' he said, a smile spreading over his face. 'Get this. Somebody from the BBC met Markey Robinson in the middle of Paris last week.'

If he had dropped a bomb it could not have caused more astonishment.

'That's a load of balls,' declared George.

In the rarefied artistic world of Belfast at that time most of the rumours and slanderous conversations originated from the third floor of Campbell's café. Here, actors, writers, artists, poets and hangers-on met to talk and eat wee buns washed down by tea or coffee. A cartoon frieze painted by Rowel Friers depicting characters like painter Willie Conor, actor Joe Tomelty, writer Sam Hanna Bell, Langtry Lynas and other luminaries snaked round the walls of the room. It was a source of amusement to visitors to hear the figures identified with a running commentary on their life styles – suitably embellished, of course. Markey's long loping figure, complete with a canvas under his arm, had its place in the cartoon. There was always somebody sitting in Campbell's. You could stay there all morning over a cup of tea without fear of being turfed out and Markey was a regular patron, although he would vanish from the scene for two or three weeks at a time.

'I was talking to some French artists on the Chance de Leesay,' he would declare on his return.

'Bollocks,' Dan O'Neill would growl, 'you've never been further than Donaghadee harbour in your life.'

Invariably, Markey would become red and indignant under his black beret and insist that he knew Paris better than Belfast. Campbell's clientele took his accounts of his wanderings abroad with a large pinch of salt and put them down to Markey's imagination. They were a source of great amusement just the same. When asked how he could afford all these foreign trips, he said it was simple. He walked down to the docks and signed on as a deckhand. Once when he claimed to have gone to the Van Gogh country around Arles, he sent us a postcard. However, even this did not silence his detractors for long. This time it was different. A person-to-person encounter. A reliable source was reporting that he had actually bumped into the man wandering around the centre of Paris. Now we did not know what to believe.

Campbell's café, Belfast

Carmel was all ears when she heard about our party. 'Now, isn't that great. Have ye invited any women?' she asked, laughing.

'Well, we'd invite you but we've only got three single beds. Who's bed would you like to share?'

'Gerard Dillon, it's an awful man ye are. The whole town would hear of it.'

'Well, if you don't tell, we won't.' Gerard rolled his eyes at her.

She giggled to herself at the thought. 'Ye'd die of fright if I said yes.' She shook her head.

'Ah, that's our hard luck. We'll have to settle for three crates of Guinness and three bottles of whiskey.'

'Mother of God, have ye invited the whole island?'

'Aye, we have,' said George.

Each of us lugging a crate of Guinness down to the dinghy starting tongues wagging among the fishermen hanging over the harbour wall. They wanted to know if we had had advance warning of another blow and offered to help us dispose of the booze any time we liked. Gerard gave them a farewell wave as I slowly rowed out of the harbour and into deep water.

Over supper we debated which night to hold the party. Early mass on Sunday morning ruled out Saturday, and Sunday was no better as the children had to be rowed to the mainland for school on Monday morning. Friday was the obvious choice. The word would soon get around.

The Lobster Pots
by Gerard Dillon

I produced the square wooden-framed reel of fishing line I had bought in Roundstone and announced my intention to catch a salmon the next day.

'Humph, salmon no less. You'll be lucky if you catch a crab,' smirked George, sending a plume of smoke from his cigarette into the air and a cascade of ash across the tiles in the hearth.

'All right,' I shot back at him, 'when Gerard and I are stuffing ourselves on salmon steaks you can watch with your tongue hanging out.'

To awaken with the sun shining like a golden orb was something we were beginning to take very much for granted. We were now into the third week without a drop of rain. The sun rose, climbed up and made its way over a cloudless arc of sky before sinking, a blood-red disc, below the horizon. It had even shone right through the blow. After breakfast George and I decided to go sketching, leaving Gerard in peace with his oils. George drew and painted watercolours at a frenetic pace. He would have a sketch finished while mine was still half-completed. I asked him if he would help me pick out some drawings and watercolours to take to Kate O'Brien's that evening and he agreed to give me a hand.

'What do you think of that oil Gerard is working on?' I asked.

'It's good. How he manages to balance those compositions of his beats me. He's much better at composing a painting than I am.'

I was surprised. That statement was the closest I ever heard George come to admitting that someone else could better him at the intricacies of picture making.

After dinner, as the other two lay sprawled on the bench in the sunshine, I announced that I was going fishing. I pretended not to hear Gerard's shout of 'mind you don't hook a shark'. They would laugh on the other side of their faces when I dished up fresh fish for supper, I said to myself.

I had thought about this fishing business and realised that I did not have the temperament for an all-day stint sitting in a boat, watching the line for a bite, so I had decided that if there were no fish wriggling on the line within ninety minutes I would head for the shore and brave the jeers of the others. In deep water a hundred yards offshore I threw the line overboard. It was a pleasant way of passing the time; the sun shone and the dinghy rocked gently as I sat with the line looped round my finger, waiting for the first jerk. After fifteen minutes I hauled up the line to check the bait. It was still there, untouched. I swung the lead-weighted line round my head and dropped it further away. A short time later I felt a tug, a tiny one, but it was gone before I could react. It came again and this time I was ready. Apply firm pressure, I thought. I did. The line tugged back. I had expected to feel the vibration of a fighting fish but this was just a firm tug. Hand over hand I hauled in the line, peering expectantly into the green depths. The bait was still on the first two hooks. My catch was on the final one, a monster crab clinging tenaciously to the bait with a pair of enormous nippers behind which multiple legs waved in all directions. This was not what I wanted. How could I fry crab? I shook the line vigorously at arm's length to send the brute back to where it belonged. It was no use. The huge claws just gripped the bait tighter. I held it well clear of the dinghy, not relishing the thought of sharing the boat with such a monster. However, I could not sit there all day and my arm was getting tired. A good belt with the oar will fix it, I thought.

To reach the oar I had to stretch and twist and turn my head to see where it was. Suddenly the line slackened and I heard a thud and the scrabbling noise of claws scraping on wood. As I turned I caught sight of the crab scuttling along the floor slats between my legs. Instinctively, I swung them up out of the way, rocking the dinghy, as the brute slithered under the stern seat, disappearing among the ropes and other junk that had accumulated there.

For a full five minutes I waited for the crab to reappear, wondering what to do next. I did not fancy the idea of rowing, with the possibility of those giant nippers crawling up my trouser leg. And there was another problem. While I had been playing mighty hunter with the crab, the dinghy had been drifting with the tide towards Roundstone. I had to start rowing. I headed back to the island harbour, with one eye on my destination and the other on the crab. There was no sign of it leaving its new lair.

As I slipped between the piers, I could see George and Gerard still outstretched on the bench. I was going to get a rough reception. Returning without a fish was bad enough but to have to admit that I had been hijacked by a monster crab would send them into hysterics. This was going to make their day. Setting my jaw, I hauled the dinghy up onto the soft sand. There was still no sign of the crab.

'Where's the salmon?' George asked, looking at my reel.

'It got away,' I lied.

That got a hoot of laughter.

'Didn't I tell you you would be lucky to catch a crab.' George was grinning all over his face.

'I did catch one and I've still got it.'

They looked at each other.

'Well, where is it?' George demanded.

'In the dinghy, waiting for one of you to take it out. It's a real monster.'

Roundstone seen from the estuary

George cast a bleary eye at me. 'Why is he talking in riddles, Gerard? I know him of old. He's up to something. What's it doing in the boat? You should have chucked it overboard.'

I told them that if I had been able to get at it, that's precisely what I would have done.

'Come on, Gerard, we're getting nowhere. Let's see what he's blethering about,' said George, heading for the beached dinghy, with Gerard and I close behind.

'I can't see any crab.' Gerard stood, hands on hips, and peered intently around the boat.

I explained that it was under the stern seat but that I would think twice about reaching in for it.

George quickly realised my predicament and laughed. 'We wondered why you were rowing so damned hard. You're a right eejit. Wait till I tell the islanders about this one.' He was enjoying my discomfiture immensely.

'OK,' I said, 'you've had your fun, now get the damn thing out unless you want its company on the trip to Roundstone tonight.'

'Get a stick,' George said. 'We can poke it out with a stick.'

Gerard found a wooden shaft and thrust it through the rubbish and into the coils of rope. A claw shot out, clamping the stick in a vice-like grip. Despite all Gerard's pushing and pulling, twisting and turning, the crab held fast.

George peered under the seat. 'God, I see what you mean. Look at the size of those nippers.'

Gerard had a flash of inspiration. 'Turn the dinghy upside down. We'll shake the bugger out. You take the bow, George, and Jim, you lend a hand here.'

As we rolled it over with a thump we could hear the rubbish rattling around. The gunwales had buried themselves in the soft sand, trapping the crab inside.

'What do we do now?'

'We'll lift it,' said Gerard. 'Jim and I will lift it. You, George, get a rock and

push it under the stern once it's clear.'

Gerard and I got ready to lift while George heaved the rock closer. I did not feel happy about pushing my fingers through the sand to get a grip but the captain had commanded.

'Ready? Lift. Come on, George, get that rock in there.'

The dinghy was a foot clear of the sand as George pushed the rock under the stern. His fingers had barely got the rock in place when he let out an almighty yell that must have been heard on the far side of the island.

'Holy suffering Jesus.' Gerard was open-mouthed and rigid. 'The crab's got George.'

It had. It clung to the fleshy part of his palm, squeezing viciously, but at least it was out of the dinghy. George danced around, emitting howls of agony, holding his arm poker stiff with the crab still dangling by one claw from his hand. We were frozen into immobility not knowing what to do.

'Get it off, you eejits. Get a stick and belt the bloody daylights out of it.'

Gerard grabbed the stick and swung round as George cavorted toward him. He raised the stick and hit the crab fair and square across its shell. George shouted with relief as it relaxed its grip, somersaulted through the air and landed between the rocks before slithering into the tide. He hunkered down, nursing his numbed hand in his armpit, and swearing harder than the proverbial trooper.

Gerard sat down beside him. 'Let's have a look at it,' he said, reaching for the injured hand.

George tried to snatch it away as his temper blew. 'Between geese, storms, starvation, drowning and now that bloody thing chewing bits off me, I'm not going to leave this island in one piece.' He was scowling and tight-lipped, with brows screwed down as he stared at his injury.

Gerard peered closely. 'You'll be all right. It's not bleeding. It's just a bit of a bruise.'

'If it was your hand you wouldn't be so bloody complacent about it.'

Poor old luckless George. Everything seemed to happen to him. He was always in the wrong place at the wrong time. Now he was in a bitter temper and nothing we could say or do would placate him, so we sat in silence and gazed at the blue ridges of the Twelve Bens, waiting for him to calm down. Eventually we coaxed him back to the cottage and settled down for a bit of desultory conversation, with Gerard and myself taking good care not to mention the subject of fish or fishing. By teatime he was more approachable, although still long in the face, but the muscles which had set rigidly round his jaw had softened and the little black moustache was beginning to perk up at the ends. Gerard and I looked at each other with relief.

I decided to sift through my drawings and watercolours for those which Kate O'Brien might appreciate. I did it without George's assistance as I felt responsible for causing his latest affliction. By the time we embarked for Roundstone, relations were back to normal and George had cheered up. He was, he declared, looking forward to a relaxed evening of excellent conversation stoked by a liberal supply of Power's Gold Label. He thought he deserved it. So did his friends.

Roundstone was slipping into its evening somnolence as we trudged past the harbour to Kate O'Brien's house, passing only the odd soul going unobtrusively about his or her business and melting into the long purple slabs of shadow laid by the sun as it slipped sideways below the horizon. Kate welcomed us at the door with a warm smile. We were not sorry to sink into the comfort of the ample armchairs in her spacious living room. It had been a long walk from the beach and it was such a warm night.

'I heard about the storm keeping you on the island. How was it?' she asked.

I glanced at Gerard but he did not respond except to shrug his shoulders.

'So it's true what the people are saying, that it did not seem to bother you much.'

'Well, our larder was running low,' Gerard answered. 'Too low. We shouldn't have let it get so empty, but by dint of improvisation, we weathered the storm. To be honest, our biggest problem was the shortage of cigarettes. We suffered agonies when the supply ran out.'

'You were lucky,' she smiled, 'that the storm ended when it did. I can't imagine you drinking nettle soup and smoking dried tea leaves.'

George leapt in. 'Four days was certainly enough for me. I can't understand how these people endure weeks of isolation in the winter. Another few days of it would have put me in the loony bin.'

Kate shook her head at him. 'You forget, George, that storms are part of life on the island. These people were born to it. They have been brought up to accept these visitations of the elements with a fortitude that would leave the likes of us floundering in a mire of anxiety and frustration.'

I thought she had hit the nail dead centre.

She looked expectantly at us. 'What would you like to drink?'

'A Guinness for me, please, Kate,' said Gerard. He was playing cautious tonight.

'The same for me, please,' I said.

George, predictably, went for a whiskey. It was like a starter's flag dropping; the horses were off. We were beginning an exciting evening of eating, drinking and crack. The change in George from his earlier petulance was unbelievable. He sparkled, driving us into fits of laughter with his stories and recollections of characters he had known in Dublin. Both he and Kate had a passion for Spain and the Spanish way of life. They were soon enthralling Gerard and me with tales of their travels in that land which, at that time, had not yet been invaded by the 'sunshine and chips' package tour industry. George had brought his guitar with him. Gerard and I had pretended not to notice it on the boat as just one comment from either of us would have resulted, while he was still in a contrary mood, in him leaving it behind on the beach.

The evening wore on, the conversation lubricated by a continual supply of Guinness and whiskey. Just as I was beginning to wonder if my head was still co-ordinated with my feet, Kate asked George to play some flamenco music on his guitar to remind her of the balmy evenings she had enjoyed in Spain. For once he needed no coaxing. He played well, although we would never have dreamt of telling him so. Soon he was strumming and finger-tapping his way through his repertoire, head bent low and cocked to one side, oblivious of everything except the music. We listened, entranced, conjuring up visions of haughtily profiled gypsies, their staccato heels clicking and exotically coloured dresses swirling. Kate was ecstatic in her appreciation of George's playing. In fact, so were Gerard and myself. This was George the extrovert in full swing, highly entertaining and marvellous company.

After a while, to my relief, Kate announced that supper was ready. I needed some food to soak up the liquor and slow down the spin in my head. Large sandwiches filled to bursting with all manner of tasty things gave full range to my natural greediness. I did justice to the sandwiches and still had room for a generous slice of chocolate cake (the sight of which had had me drooling as I worked on the savouries). I thought I would split my seams. After such a prolonged spell of exposure to our own culinary efforts, it seemed like manna.

When supper was over I brought out my drawings and watercolours for Kate to examine, saying tentatively, 'You asked to see some of my sketches so I've brought a few that might interest you.'

Actually, I had brought fifteen. Carefully, she spread them across the table under the lamp. Her silence as she examined each in turn began to worry me. I started to feel like a fool for even thinking she might like any of my scrawls and as the pile diminished without comment my panic and embarrassment increased. Finally, she gave a little sigh and put the last one down. With her face expressionless, she slid off her spectacles and leaned back in her chair.

'I like all of them, James, particularly the line drawings. Some of those are very fine indeed.'

I heaved a sigh of relief and when I turned to look at the others I saw that they were grinning like a couple of Cheshire cats. Turning back to Kate, I saw that she had picked out three of the sketches.

'I'd like to have these, James. How much do you want for them?'

For a moment I was flummoxed. I had hoped she might take one. Three was more than I had dreamt of. I stammered out a price of ten shillings, which was dismissed immediately as far too little. Kate then opened her handbag, rummaged in her purse, and taking my hand, pressed into it three one-pound notes and a ten-shilling note. I opened my mouth to protest that she was paying me too much, but she anticipated me.

'Not another word, young James. They are worth every penny.'

She had been more than generous, extravagant, in fact, but she did look genuinely pleased with her purchase. If she considered that she had got a bargain, I was not going to complain. The money would be very useful. It would help with my share of the expenses for the party and would come in handy for when I got back to Belfast. Being penniless was a state that I was well used to living with but at least I would go home from here with enough material to keep me painting for a couple of years.

Afterwards it was Kate's turn to entertain us with her stories of working as a journalist in London and as a secretary in New York. She told a good yarn and, indeed, so did both Gerard and George. I just sat and listened as the talk bounced around like a rubber ball, a non-stop marathon that never slowed down. It was only when the muffled chimes of a clock striking twelve impinged upon me that I realised that three hours had gone like three minutes. I could hardly believe that the time had flown so quickly and the evening was not yet over. George had been consuming a steady trickle of Power's Gold Label without any sign of it having any effect except to enhance his affable mood. Gerard had beamed all evening on a steady diet of Guinness. He obviously did not want a repeat of the consequences of our first visit — much to my relief.

It was one o'clock when we finally said our goodbyes and set off on the long walk back to the dinghy. There was little or no moon, so we trudged along in pitch blackness. The town centre was asleep, swathed in deep shadow, and our noisy footsteps stirred the eerie quiet in the huddle of houses. Not that our feet were the only things making a noise. George and Gerard had to conduct their usual *post mortem* on the evening's entertainment, going over and over any titbit that they thought should have been embellished or probing the tantalising glimpses that Kate had given of her short-lived marriage. She had made only a very brief reference to this and passed on without making any attempt to elaborate. I think the two of them — but Gerard in particular — loved to poke around in the enigmatic tapestry of other people's lives. They did a lot of pondering over the little bits and pieces that people let slip on such an evening as this but I don't think they were any the wiser in the end.

By the time we got to the beach our night vision had improved. This was just as well as Inishlacken was barely visible as a hump of slightly blacker darkness against the darkness of the sea, with occasional glimpses of the foam-tipped breakers as they died on the rocks. Unlike our first night crossing, at least we now knew where to look for the harbour entrance and soon saw the hard line of the wall guiding us there.

George said little on the way over. We were acutely aware of his dislike of crossing in darkness and this evening had been the worst. Only the slap of the oars striking water broke the silence as we breasted the slight ocean swell. Poor George was now even more apprehensive of the sea since his disastrous attempt at swimming.

'Well, we made it,' said Gerard as he leapt overboard to drag the dinghy up onto the soft sand. 'George, you look like a man glad to be on terra firma again.'

'I don't fancy having a hundred feet of dark water beneath me on a night as black as pitch,' retorted George.

The island lay still and silent except for the slap of the waves, and since they

were always present, they did not count. There was not a breath of wind and the scent of burning turf hung in the air. We soon had candles and oil lamps brightly burning and sank exhausted into our chairs. Gerard mustered enough energy to drop hunks of turf onto the flame dancing feebly across the embers of the fire. My head, eyes heavy with sleep, began to droop as the effort of rowing combined with the food and drink took their toll. I felt myself sliding into unconsciousness, barely hearing Gerard telling me to go to bed. I had just about enough strength to crawl into bed as the clock showed three o'clock. It was long past my noddy time.

It was broad daylight when I opened my eyes to look at the cracks zig-zagging across the ceiling. I wondered what time it was but it took me a while to reach for my wristwatch hanging from the head of the bed. Ten past ten. There was not a sign of life, not a sound – which was hardly surprising as the other two would have hit their beds long after I had. About an hour later, as I slipped out of the cottage, there was still no sign of life apart, that is, from the cacophony of snores reverberating round the walls. The air smelt of salt and the ebbing tide. There was no water in the harbour except for a ripple or two sparkling in the sun at the entrance, and over on the mainland the sun glinted on the roofs of Roundstone. To the west the sea spread toward the horizon with only a solitary fishing boat encroaching on its immensity.

I turned up the hill leading past old Séamus's cottage and in the distance I could see him poking around his turf stack, probably filling up his basket to last the day out. A few minutes later I leaned over his wall and told him that if he was thinking of visiting our cottage, he would find the lads still in bed. I explained that we had gone to Kate O'Brien's the previous night and were late home, and that the other two had stayed up even later. I asked him if he was coming to our party.

'Oh, don't fret about me. I'll be there.'

'Any time after eight o'clock, Séamus. The crack should be good.'

I continued on my way to the other side of the island and in a little saucer of beach rimmed with rocks, facing the Atlantic, my eye was drawn by the movement of a figure humping a laden kelp basket on his back as he picked a passage through the boulders. He was accompanied by a little black and white dog which yelped a greeting when it saw me. I waved to the man as I plodded on to look at the forlorn row of deserted cottages lining the track. The jumble of triangular gables outlined against the sky and the windowless holes in the walls were a sad reminder of the decline of the island but they would, nevertheless, make a good subject for a drawing. A while later I caught sight of Pádraig's familiar figure toiling his way up a steep incline. He turned and waited for me to catch up.

'Well, I see ye're out on your own this morning,' he observed.

I explained again that we'd had a late night in Roundstone and that I hadn't a clue what time the other two finally got to their beds and that they were still in them. I asked if there was any sign of the *poitín*. There was – two bottles of the best dew. I asked him what we owed him and his reply of one pound for the two bottles seemed cheap enough. I gave him the money and asked him to bring them with him on Friday night.

'Will you be bringing your wife, Pádraig?' I enquired.

He peered sideways at me. 'Oh no, she'll hardly be there.' He hesitated and then continued. 'I don't think the women will be visitin' ye. Too many men there for their liking.'

I gathered from this exchange that this was another instance where island custom differed from what I was used to. The party was evidently going to be an all-male occasion, rather like when the men would gather in the public bar while the women went to the saloon bar.

'What about the others?' I enquired. 'Did you mention the party to them?'

'Oh aye, they're looking forward to it.'

'I went fishing yesterday,' I said, changing the subject, 'but the only thing I caught was a crab. I must have been using the wrong bait.'

I had enough wit, for once, not to mention the fiasco of George and the belligerent crustacean, as I didn't think that he would appreciate being the butt of all the cracks and jokes that would ensue if the islanders got wind of that tale.

'And where did ye do your fishing?' Pádraig wanted to know.

'About a hundred yards straight out from the harbour in line with the schoolhouse,' I answered.

He shook his head and pointed over his shoulder. 'Try the opposite side facing the mainland, lad. When the tide sweeps through the channel it stirs up food for the fish. What were ye using for bait?'

He shook his head again when I told him I had just knocked a couple of limpets from a rock. He pushed his duncher back, revealing a tuft of hair, and scratched his forehead. The cap had left a crease in the greying, brown mop that circled his head. There was twinkle of merriment in his eyes as he pushed his cap back in place. He was not impressed with my bait and took me down among the seaweed-covered rocks. Brushing the weed aside, he pointed to a black shell which was sticking to a rock. Instructing me to poke out the insides and tie a wee piece of seagull feather to them, he promised me I'd catch more than a crab. I still wasn't sure I had the patience for fishing.

I remembered that I should be getting back to the cottage soon as it was my day to cook. Before leaving I double-checked with Pádraig that the geese were safely in.

He laughed. 'Ye'll be all right. I never saw a moving thing.'

After bidding him goodbye, I stayed for a while to do some sketching but with the thought of having to cook that day's dinner, I could not settle so I soon gave up the idea and made my way back to the cottage. Gerard and George were up and about by this time, seemingly no worse for their excesses of the previous evening.

After our meal we lounged about on the bench outside, soaking up the afternoon sunshine. We needed to go to Roundstone to stock up supplies again, but for the moment none of us felt inclined to move. Eventually, however, we set off. Gerard and I had offered to make the trip alone, allowing George to rest, but he was adamant that he wanted to come too. As usual I did the rowing while George sagged in the stern and Gerard, his duncher pulled low over his eyes, stretched himself out on the bow seat.

The sun beamed and the Twelve Bens shimmered in the haze as we slid smoothly out of the harbour with only a slight swell rocking the dinghy. George and Gerard had become so used to me being the ferryman that they seldom offered to row any more although there was a second set of oars aboard. I liked rowing and enjoyed the exercise, and now that the skin on my palms had hardened, I had no tender spots to bother me. We made steady progress across the channel and were soon past the halfway mark. The two gentlemen said little, being content to doze to the accompaniment of the

creaking of rowlocks and oars and the gentle burbling of the water as it creamed past the bow.

Most journeys to Roundstone and back gave us a sighting of some seals but the initial interest they had aroused in us had become sated by familiarity and nowadays we paid them scant attention. But today by the rocks, just off the island, there were lots of them all bunched together. I drew Gerard's attention to them and he pushed himself up onto one elbow to give them a casual glance before relapsing again into a more comfortable position. I glanced over my shoulder to make sure the current was not drifting us wide of our beach and in doing so I noticed three letters slide out of Gerard's folded jacket that he had forgotten to post the previous day.

I listened to his grunts as he twisted himself round to retrieve his mail. Gerard wrote a fair number of letters each week and got about the same number back. He enjoyed writing them. For my part I was very curious as to their content. I was sure that graphic descriptions of our doings of the past few weeks were being sent to all and sundry.

Suddenly, my musings were interrupted by a gulping sound from behind and I turned to look at Gerard. I asked him what was wrong but there was no answer and I stopped rowing to turn around to see what had disturbed him. He was staring, open-mouthed, off to port. I followed his gaze and froze, nearly dropping the oars overboard in sheer fright. A couple of hundred yards away an enormous triangular fin sliced through the waves, heading straight toward us. A shark!

Old Séamus had often scared the living daylights out of George by feeding us tales of shark fishing by the local men, when the creatures would flip over the currachs or even bite holes in their tarred sides. Anything I knew about them had been gleaned from films about the war in the Pacific, when the crews from torpedoed ships were chopped up by marauding sharks. Now Gerard and I sat mesmerised by the sight of that sinister fin.

The change in the motion of the dinghy brought George out of his doze and he sat up and grunted. 'Why have we stopped?' he demanded.

There was a moment of silence as he followed our gaze and then he let out a wild shriek of terror. The dinghy rocked violently as he scrambled, panic-stricken, for the seat in front of me and grabbed the second set of oars. In his haste to get them into the rowlocks he missed completely, and then when he did manage to get them fitted he did not wait for them to dip deeply enough. They skimmed the wave crests, sending showers of cold water over us. The dinghy, of course, rolled even more violently.

'George, for Christ's sake, take it easy. You're going to ditch us over the side,' Gerard yelled from the bow.

It was a waste of breath. In his panic nothing registered with George but the need for a headlong dash for the beach. There was no rhythm in his rowing. He was using short strokes and making no attempt to stay in time with my oars. Inevitably we clashed, locking our oars together.

'George, will you wait a minute. Take your time, for God's sake.'

The dinghy was rocking so violently now that I was beginning to lose my head.

'Will you just hold on a bloody minute.' I slipped the oars, leaned forward, and grabbed his shoulders, forcing him to slow down. 'Take a deep breath,' I told him.

'Where the hell is it now?' he cried, with desperation in his voice, as his eyes swivelled frantically from one side of the boat to the other.

Now that we were both resting our oars, the dinghy rolled gently with the swell while the three of us twisted and turned, trying to catch sight of that menacing shape in the water.

'It's gone. Where the hell is it?' Gerard shouted as he stared at the empty sea. George had lapsed into silence. His face was drawn, his eyes almost popping out of their sockets, and long strands of black hair straggled across his forehead. A bead of sweat trickled down one cheek. He was scared witless. So was I. We tried to persuade George to change places with Gerard but he sat still, gripping the oars as though his life depended on them, and he gave no indication of having heard a word we said. Then he started to row. He had a short, irregular rhythm that I was convinced would exhaust him in a few minutes but I had no choice but to fall in with him if we were to get anywhere at all.

'Come on, come on, we can't sit here waiting for the bloody thing to attack us,' he panted, intent on nothing but reaching dry land before the shark had time to set its sights on us again. He kept up his short-stroke rhythm and I struggled to match him. Remonstrating with him was useless but as well as exhausting him, this stroke was actually slowing us down.

Meanwhile, Gerard was keeping a wary eye on the sea. He was no happier with the situation than I was but neither of us thought that the dinghy was in any immediate peril – at least we hoped not. The real danger lay in the possibility of George going berserk and upsetting the boat if the shark reappeared. I hoped that he would soon tire himself out but he showed no sign of that. Eventually the beach came into full view, only about half a mile away, but George continued to row as if the devil was perched on his shoulder. I suddenly remembered our first attempt at rowing across, when George had complained volubly about the damage the oars were doing to his tender palms and how it would have an adverse effect on his guitar playing. He had not touched an oar since. Until now.

A sudden screech from him startled us. 'Jesus Christ, it's back again.'

The shark was indeed tracking across our stern at an angle, heading for Roundstone harbour. I had thought George was working at maximum speed before but I now discovered that I was mistaken. From some hidden reserve he managed to drag up enough energy to increase his stroke and we fairly flew through the water, leaving a swirling wake. It now became obvious that the shark was steadily drawing away from us. I yelled to George to ease up. He did not want to hear me. Turning to take a quick look over my shoulder at the beach, I saw Gerard slowly shaking his head. I knew that if he and I had made this trip alone, this mad headlong flight would not have happened and I could not envisage the state George would be in when eventually we did make land. To think that we had offered to let the wee sod stay behind to enjoy a lazy afternoon on the bench in the sun — but he had insisted on coming with us. I knew that the minute he had recovered from his fright, all hell would be let loose.

The dinghy hit the beach with a solid thump. George was out of it in one leap and sprawled on the sand above the high-water mark in an exhausted heap. He lay flat on his back, motionless except for his heaving chest. Gerard stood over him while I hauled the dinghy up onto the beach.

'Are you OK, George?' asked Gerard.

George sat up, staring at the strait between the beach and Inishlacken. 'Did it not occur to you two eejits that that damned thing could have overturned the dinghy?' he demanded, with a determined tilt to his jaw that I knew was a sure sign of mounting ire.

'Ach, George, it wasn't even close to us,' said Gerard, kicking a spray of sand impatiently. He was getting thirsty.

George glared at him. 'It was on one side of us, then it disappeared and came up on the other side. It didn't fly during the time it was out of sight.' He was livid that this thought did not appear to have dawned on either of us.

Gerard's hackles began to rise. 'The last sighting we had of the shark, it was headed for Roundstone. You were acting like it was ten feet away and coming straight for us. Your imagination was just working overtime as usual. Anyway, how come you were able to row like that. I thought rowing damaged those lily-white hands of yours.'

George studied the palms of his hands as if he had just realised their existence. There were red patches across the centres and blisters were already beginning to show. He flexed them, wincing as he stretched the damaged skin. 'God, that's all I need. I'll not be able to play the guitar for a month.'

'Well, if you had stayed put as we wanted you to, those blisters wouldn't be there.'

Gerard ought to have known better. It was like pouring petrol onto a smouldering fire.

'So it's my fault that there's a bloody great shark out there? You wanted me to stay put like a bloody hermit while you two went pub-crawling in Roundstone. Thank God I'll be back in Dublin next weekend. You can have the bloody dinghy and the bloody island to yourselves then.'

'Oh, come on, you're making a mountain out of a molehill,' said Gerard indignantly. 'We only asked if you'd like to stay behind because we thought you'd be glad of the rest.'

'Why am I always at the wrong end of the stick? I'm bloody fed up! There's a jinx running after me on this island,' said George in anguished tones.

I had to admit that he had a point. Misfortune seemed to have dogged him and he was furious, yet again, at this latest mishap.

Gerard sat down beside him on the sand. 'It was just a bit of bad luck, George. Come on, a jar or two at Connolly's will sort you out and we'll ask in the store for something for those blisters.'

George just sat there, as immovable and as uncommunicative as a rock. Gerard looked at me with a long face, obviously undecided on how to deal with this latest débâcle that had sunk George once more into a black temper, convinced of the imminent arrival of the final catastrophe which would extinguish his flame.

'Well, we can't sit here all day. We have things to get in Roundstone. Are you going to wait here until we get back?' asked Gerard.

George, having decided to be even more cussed and bloody-minded than usual, ignored him. Gerard and I sat there trying to work out our next strategy. Then we heard the sound of approaching voices. Two islanders topped the sand bank, striding toward their currach. They were laughing. The cows flicked their tails and twitched their ears as the newcomers ploughed through the sand which was liberally splattered with cow pats.

'Well, lads, are ye coming or going?' they greeted us.

'We've just got here,' said Gerard, 'but we had a problem on the way across.'

'The devil ye did. What sort of problem?'

George suddenly found his tongue. 'A bloody great shark.'

'Ach, it would be just basking shark. They won't do ye a bit of harm.' They dismissed the incident as though it were a daily occurrence. 'They get inquisitive. Just leave them be and they'll not trouble ye.' They could see the doubt on our astonished faces. 'It's the truth. It's just the sound of your oars that makes them come up to see what the racket is about.'

The thought crossed my mind that if that were true, then George must have startled every shark for a hundred miles around.

George was unconvinced. 'Are you sure it's safe to cross with a monster like that about?' His voice was laden with anxiety.

'Ach, they're more scared of ye than ye could ever be of them. The only time they might be dangerous is if ye try hooking them and ye wouldn't be trying that now, would ye?'

'Not on your life,' said George feelingly.

For once Gerard and I were in wholehearted agreement with him.

'There ye are then. Ye need niver give sharks another thought.'

George let out a long sigh of relief, and suddenly I realised why he had had the black dog on his shoulders. It was the thought of the return journey that had scared him witless. Gerard and I had been so disgusted by his performance that we had not stopped to think about going back. I wondered if George would have stayed on the mainland had we not chanced to meet the two islanders. We could sense the gloom lifting from him as we watched the two men raise their currach, and with it inverted above their heads, trudge towards the sea like a monstrous black beetle with four legs marching under its body.

'Hey, lads, will we see you at the party on Friday night?' Gerard called after them.

Their reply, coming from inside the body of the currach, was so muffled that we could not make it out, but the great bow of the craft bobbing up and down was answer enough and we collapsed in a heap laughing.

'A right pair of wags, those two,' said Gerard. 'We must look after them well on Friday.'

The currach was launched and the men waved to us. The sun caught the spray blowing across the bow as it skittered over the breakers. George stood watching them speed across the channel, heading straight as an arrow for Inishlacken. Gerard and I stood behind him, knowing full well what was going through his head as he watched the diminishing black dot on the sea. When he turned he seemed surprised to find us still standing there.

'Well, I hope those two have put your mind at rest,' said Gerard.

George shook his head. 'No, I will never be able to relax in that dinghy again. How can you two take it so calmly?'

'What do you mean?' I answered. 'How do you know how we felt? I tell you, the hair on my head stood up like bristles on a yardbrush when I first saw that fin. After that I was so busy trying to keep my oars clear of yours that I had no time to worry about the bloody shark. Then, when I saw that it was heading away from us, I thought even less about it and concentrated on not letting you capsize us. Now I feel like a drink.'

'Well, despite what those fishermen said, I still think we'd be asking for trouble if we antagonised one,' George went on.

'Speaking for myself, that's the first one I've ever seen and it can go home and tell its mates that I promise not to upset any of their tribe,' I said.

'I've heard the islanders talk about them often enough but they usually run into them well out to sea on their fishing trips,' said Gerard. 'Come on, let's get moving.' As he stood he sank up to his ankles in the soft sand, throwing the shopping bag over his shoulder. 'First stop Connolly's for medicinal reasons, then we'll get something for George's blisters.' We had not gone far when he stopped suddenly. 'What did you think of his performance, Jim? For someone who has not touched an oar since he arrived, he certainly made up for lost time.'

I could hardly believe my ears. We had just eased George out of one of his blackest moods and here was your man stirring it up again. I hardly dared look in George's direction. He looked slightly embarrassed – not much, just a fraction; he was not a man who suffered overmuch in that way. Then a slow smile edged up the corners of his moustache.

'You have to admit that that was our fastest crossing ever. Rest assured there will be no repeat. That was my last public performance.'

'Good, I'll hold you to that,' I said. 'If I'm doing the rowing at least I won't have to keep my eyes on the threshing machine in front of me.'

Gerard's eyes twinkled as he said, 'Think of the stories you'll have to tell when you get home. Your audience is likely to die laughing.'

George dug him in the shoulder. 'You're not a bad hand at spinning yarns yourself.'

'If you ask me, you're both dab hands at holding the floor,' I snorted. 'I've never known two fellows who could spout for hours about damn all the way you two can.'

'Will you listen to him! The fella who hardly ever opens his mouth and when he does it's only to say he's going to bed so he can rise with the lark.'

We ambled past the chapel at the edge of the town, stopping at the top of the hill to gaze across the harbour at the blue humps of the Twelve Bens splitting the horizon. It was a panorama that knocked the breath out of us. It was always changing. Clouds chased shadows and patches of light into moving patterns that rippled out to the horizon.

Connolly's bar was, for once, deserted and Carmel seemed glad to have our hot and thirsty company, especially Gerard's. George and I sprawled on the bench, watching as he chatted her up.

'I've just thought of something, George,' I said. 'If those sharks were so harmless, why were the seals racing about as though the fear of God was in them?'

He looked at me as though checking whether or not I was serious. The ash from his cigarette fell to the floor. 'I know just how they felt,' he said.

'Well, it's over and I'll bet you we never see another.'

It was an accurate prediction. We never did see another black fin but George was always ill at ease on subsequent crossings. He would sit stiffly upright, his eyes continually scanning the channel.

Connolly's was a cool haven from the sunshine that scorched the pavements outside. We were tempted to stay longer nursing our Guinness, but eventually we had to leave as we had our supplies to collect and George's hands needed attention. However, we left a good deal more cheerfully than we had arrived and the store across the road soon provided balm for the crimson weals across George's palms. It wasn't long before we had the grocery bags full, and I found that the Guinness had, of course, brought on my usual hunger pangs so I had plenty of incentive to make a quick crossing.

No man-of-war ever had a more vigilant crew than ours as I rowed across, with Gerard and I splitting our attention between the sea and George. For once he did not fall asleep but sat erect and alert until we were within a hundred yards of the harbour. We heaved a communal sigh of relief as we stepped ashore.

After supper we sprawled exhausted on the bench outside and watched the brilliant disc of the sun as it hovered on the horizon. There was no wind and the smoke from my pipe spiralled straight upwards while the fragrance from the wild flower patch soothed our shattered nerves. I felt a sense of contentment and hoped that the series of disagreements and upsets that had dogged us for the past two weeks was over.

George's eyes flicked about as though he was struggling to avoid closing them in sleep and the sun glinted off Gerard's bald head, where wisps of hair had settled over one ear and a gentle snore fluttered the edges of his moustache. Even the cat was sleeping.

I was just considering going for a walk when my attention was caught by the sight of two islanders walking towards the currachs on the beach. I watched as they heaped stones into a circle which they then filled with driftwood and paper, and in minutes a fire was licking round the stones. I was intrigued as to why they would want a fire on an evening like this so I dandered down to find out. By the time I reached them they had a large iron pot balanced on top of the fire and they had pulled one of the currachs alongside it. I asked them what they were doing and if they'd mind if I watched them. One of the men explained that they were boiling up lumps of tar to recoat the currach. As he talked the pipe in his mouth waggled up and down; he took it out to spit a stream of tobacco juice over the grass.

The fire needed continual replenishing with driftwood and the tar bubbled and spat as it melted. Then a long-handled brush like a floor mop was swirled around the pot and a hefty dollop of molten tar dumped onto the currach, and in no time a thick skin spread quickly the length of the boat. Watching the process, the thought came to me that if I had been aware on our first trip across to the island, complete with luggage, of just how flimsy the currachs were, I might have had more sympathy with George's uneasiness. That shining black skin was all that had been between us and a watery grave.

Footsteps behind me announced the arrival of the other two, who had also been bitten by curiosity.

'You made a late start on that job,' said Gerard.

'Ah no, this is the right time of the evening for it,' one of the men replied. 'It's cool now. The afternoon sun would melt the ass off ye, and the tar would never dry.'

George and Gerard walked round the currach, inspecting the workmanship. The men assured them that it would be ready for use the next day. George, of course, was not much impressed by the seaworthiness of tarred canvas over a light frame, especially in the mighty seas around Inishlacken, and we stood in the soft evening light discussing the efficacy of currachs. The island men were emphatic that they felt safer in the currach than they would in our dinghy and said it was more seaworthy in rough weather than the heavy wooden boat. I tended to be persuaded by them. After all, they were professionals expressing an opinion which they backed with their lives every day and whose ancestors had done the same for a thousand years and more.

Later we returned to the cottage and sat round the turf fire drinking mugs of tea as the paraffin lamp cast deep shadows in the corners of the room.

'Tomorrow,' I announced, 'I'm going to see Bulmer Hobson.'

The two of them groaned in unison.

'Jesus, how many times have we heard that?' said Gerard.

'I'm telling you,' I said, unfazed. 'Tomorrow, I'm going. I've got to go. I bet you that the first person I meet when I get back to Belfast will be old W.R. Gordon and his first question will be, "Did you go to see Bulmer Hobson?" He lives along the Clifden road. I'll find him tomorrow.'

I paused for effect and they both started up in a singsong voice, 'I'll see Bulmer in the morning.' Then they fell over laughing at their own wit but I had some information that would split their gobs from ear to ear.

'Oh, I forgot to tell you. Pádraig says he can get us two bottles of *poitín* for a pound.'

'God,' said George 'that's value for money. A man could get pissed out of his mind on that.' From the expression in his eyes it was clear that he was already sampling the mountain dew in his imagination.

'Gerard, have you invited the women to this party of ours?' I asked.

'Women – don't be daft. It's a drinking party. What the hell put that idea into your head?' There was no doubting George's opinion on the subject.

'Well,' I said, 'Gerard said we were throwing a party for the islanders and I just wondered.'

'They wouldn't come even if they were asked,' Gerard said quietly. 'Don't ask me why because I don't know, but they wouldn't.'

I remembered the puzzled look on Pádraig's face when I had asked him if his wife was coming. It was just as well, I thought, where would we have put them? There was going to be barely enough room in the cottage anyway. George and Gerard looked set to talk half the night away yet again but I was, as usual, ready to keel over with sleep. I rose and shuffled to the door.

'Good-night, I'm off to bed. I'll try not to wake you in the morning.'

I might as well have been talking to the wall for all the notice they took.

6

A bright morning sky gave the promise of another beautiful day when I awakened. I was still determined to see Bulmer Hobson. Somebody would tell me where he lived and I decided to arrive unannounced in the hope that he would be at home. I was ready to depart when the other two appeared, but I offered to boil the kettle for them.

'Do you want toast with your eggs?' I asked.

They looked at me with the disgust that the late riser has for the early bird.

'Why is he always so energetic first thing in the morning?' demanded George.

'Too much red blood in him – not like that amber stuff of yours,' said Gerard with a grin. 'When will you be back?'

'I don't know. It all depends on how long it takes me to find his house and what happens when I get there. Middle of the afternoon, I suppose.'

So I set off and soon Inishlacken was retreating behind the dinghy as I rowed myself across to the mainland. I enjoyed the trip: the physical effort of moving the boat through the water, the silence broken only by the chuckle of the bow wave and the sun glinting off the swirl of froth behind the stern. On the shore a clutch of cows stood motionless in a stone-walled patch of green, watching me glide past, and a lone figure struggled up from the beach bowed under the weight of a wicker basketload of seaweed. I watched him disappear over the ridge. It was an empty sea – not even the fishing boats were out.

Half an hour later I was striding past the chapel on the Clifden road. Somewhere ahead was Bulmer Hobson's house. As I climbed the hill I stopped for a breather, and looking out across the sea, I was surprised to see how far away the island was. The hill seemed to get steeper. Further along, on the bend of the road, a head appeared, followed by shoulders, then half a body pedalling a bicycle. With a visible sigh of relief, the body sat upright as it topped the hill and started freewheeling at speed toward me. I waved him down and his brakes squealed against the rims as he shuddered to a halt beside me. I wished him good morning and asked if he knew where Bulmer Hobson's house was. He did. It was just round the next bend and I couldn't miss it. He pushed off, put his feet on the pedals and sped down the hill. I went on round the bend to find Hobson's bungalow facing the road. Now that I was here and walking up the path to his door, I began to worry about what I was going to say when I met him.

'Excuse me, I'm sorry to bother you, but is this Mr Bulmer Hobson's house?' I asked the woman who opened the door.

She nodded.

'My name's James MacIntrye from Belfast. A friend of mine, W.R. Gordon, asked me to call on Mr Hobson to give him his best regards.'

'Would you like to come in and see him yourself?' she said, quietly ushering me in.

I found the great man huddled deep in a armchair. He was old, late sixties or early seventies, I guessed. A huge magnifying glass was suspended on a pulley over a table littered with books from which he was making lengthy notes. I was face to face with Bulmer Hobson at last. As if by magic, cups of tea appeared and I could see from the way his fingers fumbled over the teacup that his sight was bad. Not his mind, however, for I was soon fielding a barrage of questions. What was W.R. Gordon doing with himself now that he had retired? W.R., who had been an art teacher at the Royal Belfast Academical Institution, was now devoting his time to his own paintings.

'What about the theatre – he had a passion for the theatre?' Hobson asked.

I had no idea. I did not know of his interest or what form it took. That was just the beginning. In the next few hours a lot more would be divulged that would open my eyes to the artistic life of the city. Belfast, it transpired, was a source of fascination to him. He asked about the theatre, books, artists and art exhibitions. He extracted titbits of information from me that I did not know I possessed.

It was a long while before I was able to turn the conversation round to himself. He had been born in Holywood, County Down, of Quaker parents and educated at Friends' School in Lisburn. After leaving school he had become a disciple of Wolfe Tone and a member of various nationalist societies. My knowledge of Southern Irish politics was only marginal but it was soon apparent that he had been a revolutionary, a hunted man with a price on his head, although he did not say so outright.

My father had been in the Royal Irish Constabulary until partition, when he joined the Royal Ulster Constabulary. I wondered what he would have to say when I told him whom I had met in Roundstone. The 'republicans', as he called them, had given the RUC a rough time in Belfast over the years.

Hobson had set up the Protestant Nationalist Society in 1900 to recruit young Protestants into the nationalist movement. In 1907 he had gone to America to introduce the Sinn Féin movement there; a founder member of the Irish Volunteers in 1913, he had organised the landing of illegal arms at Howth in 1914. No wonder everyone in and around Roundstone knew of him.

He had withdrawn from the revolutionary movement after the 1916 rising but when the Free State was formed in 1922 he was appointed head of the Revenue Commissioners' Stamp Department. He had settled in Roundstone when he retired in 1948. At various stages of his life he had edited magazines and written books and articles. He was presently writing an account of his early years, which explained why his table was littered with notes and books.

He stopped talking about himself abruptly and began to question me about

Gerard and George. He seemed very curious about them. What subjects did they paint? How often did they exhibit and what did they think of Inishlacken and Roundstone? When he took off his glasses to dab his eyes, I saw that they were the palest of blue, almost opaque, the corneas tinged a dull yellow. His spectacle lenses were as thick as milk bottle bottoms and there was a permanent, deep red weal across the bridge of his nose which served to emphasise his colourless complexion.

I sneaked a quick glance at my watch and found that we had been talking for over two hours. However, his persistent questioning was not, I thought, just nosiness but a genuine interest in our activities on and off the island. He obviously enjoyed having someone to talk to and later I was treated to a potted history of Inishlacken and Roundstone. Roundstone harbour and its stone houses had been built by a Scots Presbyterian, John Nimmo, in the early part of the nineteenth century and Hobson was of the opinion that if he were to come back now he would find the place little changed.

'Inishlacken,' he declared as he eased himself into a more comfortable position, 'once had a population of over two hundred people. Two hundred! Where in the name of God did they all live and what did they live on? That was back in 1830 and the population has declined steadily since then. Even so, that old schoolhouse had fifty pupils and two teachers in its heyday. It was closed some time in the mid-thirties. It's a bit different nowadays; there can't be more than two dozen people living on the island now and I wonder how long they will stay.'

'It's a hard life,' I said.

'Aye,' he went on soberly, 'the young ones will not put up with what their elders had to endure. They suffered some dreadful calamities. The worst was the Big Wind.'

I told him that one of the islanders had mentioned the Big Wind to me. 'It puzzled me,' I said. 'I don't remember hearing a word about it on the wireless or reading about it in the papers.'

Hobson sat deeper in his chair and chuckled. 'I'm not surprised at you not hearing about it on the wireless. The Big Wind blew in 1839.'

I wondered if he realised why I was so surprised. One of the island women had told me all about it; how the ferocious wind had stripped off most of the thatched roofs, how walls had collapsed and high tides had pounded over the beaches, throwing stones like cannon balls against the cottage walls. Some cottages had been completely destroyed. Folk had been injured, but fortunately no one was killed. This tale of woe, told with so much pathos and detail, had left me with the impression that the wind had happened fairly recently, certainly not over a hundred years ago. I saw the old man looking at me, and although he said nothing, I had a shrewd suspicion that he had shared my experience of the long memories of these people who lived so close to nature.

'I hear you were storm-bound for a few days,' he said, shuffling through the papers on his desk. 'How did you and your friends cope with that?'

I wondered if there was anything that we did that did not get relayed round the population of Roundstone sooner or later.

'I'll say one thing, Mr Hobson,' I said. 'If it had been the middle of winter with driving rain under the half-light of heavy storm clouds, I would not have enjoyed it at all.'

He nodded, stating that it took a lot of tenacity and courage to survive on the islands. He admired the people for those qualities and wished that he had been endowed with even a small part of them.

I looked sideways at him, thinking that his own life had not exactly been a humdrum one nor had it been lacking in either tenacity or courage.

'Well, it wouldn't do for me,' I said. 'I like my comforts and the conveniences of life in the city.' I went on to tell him of our problems in adjusting to island living and of the struggle we had had to make our rations last during our four stormy days. I stole another look at my watch and was seized by guilt. I had been there for hours interrupting the man. 'It's been great meeting you at last,' I said, rising to leave, 'but I think I ought to let you get on with your work.'

The words were still on my lips when the lady, whom I had presumed to be his wife but who may have been his housekeeper, swept in carrying a tray of sandwiches and cake.

'You can't leave now after I've made all these sandwiches,' she said, smiling as she cleared a space on the table.

I was suddenly as hungry as an Irish wolfhound. It had been a long time since breakfast.

As we ate he told me that the book he was working on would be called *Ireland, Yesterday and Tomorrow.* 'You'll find the story of my life in it. I hope you will read it once it gets published.'

I assured him I would.

I shook hands with him and the lady and thanked them for their hospitality, promising to take their good wishes to W.R. Gordon, and I set off to walk through the warm afternoon sunshine back to the beach. I had been gone for hours. The other two would be furious. I just hoped they had not made any plans to visit Roundstone. Woe betide me if they had. The thought prompted me to pass the beach and head straight into the village, where I picked up the mail, bought an ounce of Mick McQuaid and some sweets before trudging, sweating, back to the dinghy. A bit of a swell had got up during my absence, but in no time I was swinging the dinghy round to steer through the entrance to the harbour on Inishlacken. Out of the corner of my eye I suddenly saw a familiar figure rearing up on the high rocks overlooking my landing place. I was too far away to see the face but there no mistaking that slightly rotund figure. Gerard was looking out for me.

As I hauled the dinghy ashore, he wandered up behind me, saying, 'We were beginning to consider sending out a search party to look for your body. Where did you get to?'

'What a day! Have I got a tale to tell you and George. I was with Bulmer Hobson for hours. Here's a letter for you and one for George. Have a caramel. I needed something to chew on the way back.' I had brought them more than caramels to chew over tea.

'You mean to say he claims to have been responsible for the gun-running at Howth?' George asked with a suspicious glint in his eye.

'That and more. You should call and see him. He's a talking history book. He made history. He's a really fascinating character. The two of you should meet him.'

'I'll call and see him sometime,' said Gerard. 'But how does W.R. Gordon fit in with a larger-than-life rebel?'

'They were both involved in staging amateur productions for the theatre in their young days but I have a feeling that it's a long, long time since they last met.'

The story of Hobson's rebellious life sparked off an evening of speculation and argument. Later Gerard lifted his mail off the mantelpiece. He squinted at the handwriting and the postmark before slitting open the envelope with one finger. There was a frozen, poker-faced absence of expression on his face as he read the letter. Clearly he was annoyed about something. I had seen that look before, usually when I had committed a faux pas.

'Suffering Jesus!'

'Now what's wrong?' asked George.

'Middleton. Some bloody fool has just paid one hundred and fifty pounds for one of his oils at the Waddington.'

One hundred and fifty pounds! It was a fortune. I could live for twelve months on that.

George began to huff and puff like a train blowing off steam as he prepared to cut the tripe out of the fortunate painter. 'Bloody jack-in-the-box,' he thundered as his hand brushed his hair to one side. He saw my puzzled look. 'First it was impressionism, then pointillism, then surrealism – and now it's Jack Yeats.'

For once I managed to keep my mouth shut as I detected signs of the green-eyed monster surfacing. I did not dare mention that when I had noticed Middleton's abrupt changes of style I had been very envious of his ability to absorb and adapt to each new technique.

Gerard was now going full blast in a long tirade, ridiculing Middleton's seeming lack of single-mindedness. 'Where is the real Middleton in all this?' he asked finally.

'You mean, there is one?' was George's barbed rejoinder.

And so they went on and on. I began to fall asleep in my chair only to be jolted awake time and again by the noise they made. Eventually I slipped off to bed before George could turn his attention to me.

Friday morning dawned. Party day. The few arrangements needed for the party, chiefly the supply of booze and its distribution, had been settled. There was nothing to do. So we thought.

George, as usual, disappeared immediately after breakfast, clutching a three-day-old newspaper. When he returned fifteen minutes later he said casually, 'If there's a run on the bog tonight, it will overflow.'

Gerard's piece of crispy toast paused on its way to his mouth. His forehead creased as he absorbed this riveting piece of news. Then he bit off the corner and chomped absent-mindedly as he favoured me with a wintry look. 'You have a disposal problem,' he said.

'What do you mean, *I* have a disposal problem?' I spluttered.

'You made our tin bog so you have to solve the problem of getting rid of the contents.'

I was out-gunned. It was a dilemma. Digging a hole was out of the question. I appealed for help.

Gerard addressed George with a mock serious expression. 'George, you filled that bog by yourself. It's up to you to tell the Big Lad here where to put the contents of his masterpiece.'

George scowled at me for only solving half of our problem. 'Why not dump it over the back wall and cover it up with seaweed?'

'In this heat – it would stink us out of the house in a couple of hours,' I said.

'And you're forgetting something,' Gerard said blandly. 'The nearest seaweed is over at Pádraig's place. Do you fancy carrying a load past those geese?'

'And if we dump it in the sea the tide will wash it back up onto the beach,' I continued helpfully.

George suddenly sat up and beamed. 'Why don't we ask Michael what he does with his?'

'We discussed this before, remember, and we agreed that it was a touchy subject,' I answered.

Gerard concurred that it was indeed an awkward subject.

George brightened again. 'We'll send Jim to ask him. He's only a young buck. Michael won't mind him asking embarrassing questions.'

'I'm damned sure you won't and he will,' I cried indignantly. 'You go yourself. This time next week you'll be back in Dublin and Michael will have forgotten you asked.'

Gerard, the old smoothie, said, 'Come on, Jim, it's your bog. Tell Michael you can't see how you could dig a hole in solid rock to bury it. He'll understand that a craftsman would need local advice. See what he says.'

'Why is it that I always get the jobs that you two don't want to know about?' I put on a show of indignation and obstinacy but I knew that in the end they would wear me down, and I began to consider what I could say to Michael. No matter which way I thought to I put it I was still committed to asking him where he tipped his bucket. I was still rephrasing the question over and over in my mind as I trudged towards Michael's cottage, with the morning sun scorching the back of my neck. Soon I saw his hens jumping and flapping over his thatch. He was always chasing them off the roof because of the deep holes they dug there. There was no sign of him. I looked around but did not see him in any of his small fields. In the heat there was not a creature moving; even the sheep had huddled in the shade of the stone walls to escape the hot sun. I

began to cheer up. If Michael was not about I could head back to the cottage and confess that I had failed in my mission and now it was their turn to tackle the problem.

However, my optimism was short-lived, for Michael suddenly materialised. Walking from one of his outhouses, he rounded a corner and entered through the open door of his sea-facing cottage. I had better get it over with, I thought. I was about to shout his name when a figure appeared as if by magic. It was Michael's wife. She gave me a shy smile and a questioning look. I was bereft of my wits. For what seemed an age I struggled to find my voice to say something, anything, to get me out of this situation. Eventually, I croaked, 'Ah . . . Mrs Woods, ah . . . could you spare a dozen eggs, please?'

'I can that,' she answered, and vanished into the henhouse, leaving me rattling the pennies in my pocket and feeling like an eejit.

I had my back to the door. Footsteps sounded behind me and when I turned I found Michael filling the doorway, sucking his pipe. Of course, I should have seized the moment to ask the vital question. But I dithered, fearing that his wife would reappear at any second.

'Ye must eat a hell of a lot of eggs,' observed Michael.

'Here ye are then, fresh laid this morning. Now be careful how ye carry them,' said Michael's wife, bustling out of the henhouse with my eggs in a brown paper bag.

I smiled thinly and nodded. 'See you later, Michael,' I said and left clutching my bag of eggs and trying to hide my discomfiture.

George and Gerard were sitting sunning themselves when I pushed through the gate.

'What have you got in the bag, Jim?'

'Eggs.'

'Eggs? The place is coming down with eggs,' exclaimed Gerard. 'Why did you bring more?'

So I told them, watching in disgust as the eyes rolled in their heads and they dug each other in the ribs, splitting their sides laughing at the predicament they had placed me in.

'God, it could only happen to Jim,' hooted George.

I was incensed. 'Sod off, you shouldn't have sent me in the first place.'

After a time they calmed down and I aimed a finger at them. 'Don't worry, you won't have to exercise those useless brains of yours. I've solved the problem again.'

That made them sit up; they looked at me warily.

'I was kicking a stone along the path, wishing it was one of your heads, when it bounced into the sand and buried itself.'

I paused, waiting for the penny to drop. Eventually it did.

'You mean we should dig a big hole on the beach?' asked Gerard.

'God!' said George. 'Brains, the long string of misery has got some upstairs after all.'

Gerard beamed at him. 'You can help him dig the hole while I make the dinner.'

George's face fell instantly. Wielding a shovel might damage those delicate, artistic hands of his. He had been outmanoeuvred.

We carried the can onto the beach and very quickly buried the contents under four feet of sand, spurred on by what George graphically described as 'a scent decidedly more fruity than that of new-mown hay'. He dropped this witticism, of course, while standing six feet upwind watching me struggling with the can. Then he squatted down and watched again as I rolled two large boulders over the burial mound. These were markers for Gerard's benefit. I did not intend to dig any more holes on the beach during this holiday. I always did mean to ask Gerard how he fared in this respect during his last five months on the island but I never got around to it.

We decided to spend an hour slicing and buttering two loaves of bread to make a pile of cheese sandwiches and then we cleared the floor by pushing the table to the far end of the living room beside the dresser. The crates of Guinness and bottles of *poitín* and whiskey were stacked underneath the dresser while the sandwiches rested on the top shelf. The few chairs we possessed were arranged around the wall, and upturned Guinness

Michael Woods (left) with Gerard

crates and planks made a couple of benches. We were ready to receive our guests.

Gerard fussed about like a broody hen, anxiously anticipating any unforeseen calamities that might occur. He poked through his collection of records, picking out jigs, reels and Percy French songs. There would be no lack of music. One of the islanders had been coaxed into bringing along his fiddle and there was George and his guitar to back him up. Then Gerard began to fret about the disposal of the empties, concerned that someone might trip over them. George began to get irritated with him and told him to sit down and relax – a bit rich coming from the daddy of all fidgets and fusspots.

I wandered down to the beach. It was a balmy evening, fragrant with the salt-sea air and the seaweed tang of iodine mingling with that of burning turf. A solitary line of footsteps in the sand marked my passage along the water's edge to the end of the beach. I clambered across the rocks onto the grassy rim. To the north-west I had a grand view of the empty channel between Inishlacken and Roundstone, with the coastline filling the horizon. To the west a warm, pale yellow ball shot with streaks of orange and pink wobbled briefly and then sank beneath the waves that rose and fell all the way to America. There wasn't a boat or a ship in sight.

I suddenly noticed a movement in the channel and saw that a three-man currach was coming towards the island at a whacking rate, heading straight for the harbour. I remembered that the other day in Connolly's, when the Guinness had been flowing copiously, Gerard had extended a party invitation to some of the fishermen. It looked as though a few of them had taken him up on his offer. I watched as they landed and beached the currach upside down on the grass. One of them carried a fish so big that its head scraped through the grass as he struggled up the slope.

Their boisterous laughter brought Gerard and George to the cottage door. The man handed Gerard the fish. It was a salmon. The weight of it took him by surprise.

'Suffering Jesus,' he exclaimed, 'this thing weighs a ton.'

'It's a present for ye,' said the fisherman, laughing at Gerard's expression.

George was delighted. 'Man, that's terrific. Salmon steaks for the rest of the week.'

I knew how he felt. Eggs and toast had lost their appeal.

Gerard ushered in our first guests, and pointing to the table told them to help themselves. One by one the other guests straggled in. Some were a bit hesitant on the doorstep but once across the threshold they quickly lost their shyness. Behind the table a beaming Gerard handed out welcoming drinks.

We left the cottage door open to a black sky that was speckled with a million stars. In the still air of the evening the sounds of our merry-making echoed across the island. The party had started slowly and quietly but by midnight things had livened up. Our guests, perched on the crude benches surrounded by empty bottles, talked and laughed, their feet tapping to the accompaniment of the old gramophone working non-stop belting out background music. The story of us being terrorised by a gaggle of militant geese had by now passed into island folklore and the islanders were convulsed with laughter as the tale was retold. They bombarded us from all sides with advice on how to cope with the aggressive birds in future encounters.

I had earlier decided that I would stick to Guinness for the evening. Whiskey flattened me and I had no doubt that *poitín* would do the same thing. By this time I had sunk a good few jars but so far they seemed to be having little effect. But with the mass of bodies crammed into the small room and every inch of space occupied by standing or sitting drinkers, the sweat was running off me in rivers.

At last the fiddler, after much persuasion, put aside his glass of Guinness, ran a hand over his unshaven jaw, picked up his fiddle and hurled himself into a hectic reel. Feet banged on the stone floor, picking up the rhythm, someone started slapping hands, others pounded their knees and others gave vent to loud yells. Loosened by a few jars to wash down his whiskeys, George soon had his guitar competing with the fiddle in a mad race through a jig. Two of the men jumped up and started to dance by the door. At least that had been their intention, but their legs had different ideas. One whirl too many shot them through the door and out into the garden. The laughter from the darkness told us that no bones were broken although no one inside seem at all concerned at their fate.

The drink on the table was disappearing at a prodigious rate. There was a steady procession of men disappearing hurriedly through the door to seek the seclusion of the darkness, and with only the stars for illumination, it really was dark. Occasionally we could hear hoots of laughter as swaying bodies bounced off one another.

Initially, Gerard had been piling empties neatly by the table but events had overtaken him and now there were bottles everywhere. He gave up. Suddenly he burst into a rendition of 'The Wild Colonial Boy', which George quickly picked up on the guitar, and soon every voice in the room was trying to raise the roof. Suzy Blue Hole had taken refuge in my bedroom all evening but now she shot out through the door into the peace of the garden. I couldn't blame her. The noise was appalling.

Old Séamus had planted himself in the most comfortable seat in the room, close by the peat fire. His toothless, deeply grooved, grizzled old face was creased with laughter. The glass firmly clasped in his large bony hand had been topped up all evening. With Séamus, you never knew whether or not he was legless until he stood up. Now he was enclosed in his own world, singing his heart out, oblivious that his song was quite different to the one the rest of us were belting out. But the old boy was happy.

When the singers, exhausted by their efforts, stopped for a breather and another gulp of fuel, a voice asked, 'Do yes mind if I have a bite to eat?'

We had forgotten all about the sandwiches on top of the dresser. Gerard's voice floated out of the mêlée, telling everyone to help themselves. One of the islanders reached up and spread the plates piled with sandwiches across the table. The food began to vanish under a mass of grabbing hands. I realised that this was competition the like of which I had never encountered before and if I didn't grab a sandwich quickly, there would soon be none left. I stood up and was suddenly conscious that my legs were swaying me from side to side. The sandwiches got no nearer my groping hands, and even worse, my eyes were misbehaving as the table circled round me. I blinked furiously, shook my head and shut my eyes tight. This was a mistake. The room toppled sideways, leaving me grappling wildly for support. I crashed against the wall and slid downwards, my legs unable to support me.

'Haul him up.'

Out of the darkness I heard George's voice and wondered who he was talking about. Someone grabbed me by the arms and pulled me up into a chair.

'Here, son, get that inside ye.'

A sandwich was thrust into my hand. This was something I could cope with and my hand went through the motions of automatically feeding the face in front of it. I was aware of starting on the sandwich but after that everything got lost in an alcoholic haze. I slumped sideways, snoring my head off – or so I was told.

It seemed like hours but was probably only a short time later that someone yanked me upright in the chair, put a Guinness into my hand and said, 'This'll see ye right.' My short nap had temporarily stilled the movement of the walls and ceiling but I still felt that parts of my body did not belong to me. I asked what time it was.

'Two o'clock, it's early yet. Forget about your bed, you big eejit, the party is just getting going.'

George took me by the arm and dragged me outside where the cool night air could clear my fuddled brain.

'Come on, I'll walk you down to the harbour to sober your daft head up a bit.'

He pushed me through the garden gate and then steered me round boulders to the beach.

'Sit on that stone a minute.'

Gingerly, I sat down.

'Where's your pipe?'

With a struggle I fished it out of my shirt pocket. It was filled and ready to smoke. George lit it, tamped down the glowing tobacco and pushed it into my mouth. Obediently, I sucked. The pungent scent of Mick McQuaid wafted into the salty air and smoke began to spiral round George, who was perched on the upturned dinghy.

'Jesus, will you listen to that racket!'

Even out in the open the noise was deafening. Fiddle music brought a spasm of hand-clapping that sounded like a regiment of soldiers marching up and down our living room. I was sure that every cottage on the island must be shaking on its foundations.

'Right, on your feet, or else they'll be wondering where we've got to,' said George, hauling me upright.

We staggered back to the cottage but none of the boisterous mob seemed to have even noticed our absence. My spell in the open air had given me a second wind and I could see that there were a few in worse shape than me. I had never seen so many glowing, animated faces in my life. One old fellow kept coming to me every five minutes to shake my hand in a grip that paralysed my fingers, causing me to wonder if they would ever be fit to hold a brush again. He was as pissed as I was.

Then amid the din Gerard suddenly called for silence and turning to George, he said, 'Come on, George, now is the time for your party piece.'

George scowled at him as I pricked up my ears. This was something new to me. George shook his head but against Gerard's cajoling he didn't stand a chance.

'Come on, give us all something to remember when you have fled to the fleshpots of Dublin.'

'How about doing it yourself?' asked George.

'You know bloody rightly that I've got too much hair. Yours are much more realistic,' replied Gerard as he hauled a protesting George to his feet. 'Stop playing hard to get and I'll make you a big breakfast in the morning.'

George rolled his eyes in disgust as he picked his way reluctantly to the bedroom. Gerard whispered something to the fiddler and then followed him. The door closed behind them and I scratched my head in bewilderment. What were they up to now? I had never seen this pantomime before. Two loud bangs on the bedroom door was the signal for the fiddler to launch into a slow waltz; the bedroom door opened and Gerard strode out, throwing his arms in the air.

'Gentlemen, your attention, please. Let me present to you Mademoiselle Campbello.'

There was silence for a few seconds then, when George appeared, the roof quivered at the roar of laughter that ensued. He was naked to the waist with a towel wrapped tightly round him. We could just see his rolled-up trouser bottoms, from which emerged a pair of hairy legs with the feet jammed into boots. Above the towel, drawn in bright red poster paint on his chest muscles, was a pair of huge bosoms. This alluring picture was completed by a large circle drawn round his navel. As he began to sway to the music of the fiddler, the big red boobs danced up and down and the red dot on his belly gyrated enticingly. He swayed his hips, snaked his arms round his waist, and turned to display his backside rippling to the rhythm of the music. The room just exploded with howls of laughter. Some of the men were so convulsed that tears were streaming down their cheeks.

But George had more to give. He pouted his lips, fluttered his eyelashes, and then with a flip of one hand lifted the towel a shade more than was discreet to expose more of his hairy legs. As the music ended he cupped a hand under each breast, gave a final wiggle, and lifted his towel in a curtsey, turned and retired into the bedroom with a departing shake of his bum. What an exit! Everyone whooped, clapped and yelled for an encore, although as I looked around, the thought came to me that any more excitement might finish off some of our more ancient guests.

'I've nivir seen anything like that in me life. Wait till I tell the wife,' said one old fellow with a grin that stretched from ear to ear.

George re-emerged from the bedroom to another round of applause and a broad grin split his face. A grin broad enough to hide the hint of a blush. Someone pushed a Guinness into his hand and he took a long swig, wiped his mouth with his hand and said, 'My services, gentlemen, are yours to command. By the evening or by the hour, farewell parties, bar mitzvahs and ould Slattery's hoolies I perform, regardless of inconvenience, for money or drink – but preferably both.' He bowed deeply to his audience and sat down.

I could feel the booze begin to hit me again and was aware that some of the guests were now legless. Unable to sit upright, they sprawled on the floor.

'Them boyos is going to have trouble making the crossing to Roundstone,' said one of the islanders, poking a foot at the inert form of one of the men from the mainland.

Through the cottage window I could see daylight streaking the horizon in pale shades of lemon and pink. I could not remember the last time I had seen a summer sunrise but I was going to see one today unless the Guinness got to me first. My eyes felt like lead. George and Gerard, needless to say, were still going strong. Gerard, as animated as ever, was arguing with a couple of islanders in one corner and George was in his element, the focus of attention for four of the others around the fire.

Pádraig was sitting next to me, a boozy smile on his face as he sipped the last of the *poitín*. I asked him if he had any idea what time it was. He squinted out of the window at the light in the east, reminding me that we were on Inishlacken, where time was not all that important and did not have to be measured by a clock.

'It's time I was heading home or else I'll be crawling back,' he answered. He rose unsteadily to his feet and shouted, 'Right, lads, I'm on me way. I'm thanking the three of ye for a grand party – one we'll remember for many a year.' He stopped and focused on the recumbent fisherman from Roundstone. 'We'd best get these lads to their currach or they'll nivir make it this day.'

Eventually, by pointing out that the last drop of booze had been drunk, he managed to persuade the other two men from Roundstone to help their companion to the currach and head for home. It was not easy manhandling the nearly comatose man through the door and along the winding path, but they managed to get an arm under each of his shoulders and dragged him to the beach where he woke up and heaped abuse on everyone he saw.

I watched this performance from the bench by the cottage door and then I thought that maybe they could do with a bit of help, so I stood up and was immediately struck by the odd appearance of the sky. It seemed to be in the wrong place and then it started to fade away.

'He's bloody past reviving this time,' said George's voice from far away. 'Get his boots off and dump him on the bed.'

That was the last I remembered of the party.

It seemed only minutes later that I opened my eyes and found myself in bed still wearing my trousers, shirt and pullover. I levered myself up on one elbow and raised my head. Immediately, the walls began to spin and a blinding pain split my head in two. I slumped back on the pillow and glanced at my watch. The hands pointed to twelve thirty. It was past midday, dinnertime, and me still in bed. I could not believe it. I must have dozed off again because I was awakened by a loud thud as though someone had fallen out of bed. I listened intently but heard nothing more and decided that I must have dreamt it. Then the bedroom door opened. A bald head appeared, under which was a crumpled face as along as a Lurgan spade, and a pair of bloodshot eyes regarded me lugubriously. It was Gerard. I hoped I looked better than he did.

'You all right?' he croaked. 'Christ, I feel terrible.'

'You look it,' I said.

'Well, I notice that you aren't exactly buzzing around like a blue-arsed fly.'

'I feel bloody awful,' I said and shook my head. I instantly decided that I would never shake it again. 'Where's George?'

'Snoring like a pig. If a bomb went off he wouldn't notice.'

'What time was it when everyone finally went home?'

'Well, it was broad daylight. Must have been around five.'

'I don't remember when I went to bed or how I got there. Do you remember?'

'We dumped you in bed about three or a bit after. You were plastered by then so we had to get you out of harm's way.'

'What about the men from Roundstone? How did they get home? I remember one of them was really pissed.'

'He'll be the one who fell out of the currach before they got all of him aboard.' Gerard gave a flicker of a smile at the memory. 'Sitting in the tide sobered him up quick enough. They were all three singing their heads off as they rowed out of the harbour.' He slumped down on my bed. 'God knows what time it was when they arrived – or even if they did. I think fishermen are like homing pigeons; no matter what state they're in they can find their way home. Old Séamus passed out on my bed. He was really soused. Two of the islanders carried him home.' Gerard started to shake his head, changed his mind and buried it in his hands instead. 'I think everybody enjoyed themselves but there will be a lot of sore bonces around today.' He levered himself slowly and carefully off the bed and wiped his forehead with the back of his hand, smoothing the sparse hairs behind his ears. 'Even the thought of eating gives me the shudders.'

I did not even dare to nod in agreement. 'Well,' I said, 'I think I'll drag myself outside for a bit. Maybe fresh air and a bit of sun will bring on a cure.'

About an hour later I heard a grunt and the thump of a body hitting the grass beside me. I opened one eye and looked at George. He reeked like a brewery.

'What the hell were you drinking last night? I can smell you from here,' I said by way of greeting.

'Shut up. I'm in no mood for talking.'

'Well, that's a change,' I said sarcastically.

When he did not rise to the bait I took a hard look at him. He lay on his back as inert as a lump of dough and about the same colour. The party had taken the *joie de vivre* from all three of us. None of us had the slightest inclination to venture even as far as the garden gate and nobody had an appetite – not even me. The mere mention of food produced a collective shudder. As the sun went down, my head still felt as though it had rocks in it and I was back in bed as soon as it was decently dark. If the other two noticed my departure, they said nothing. There were no midnight arguments around the fire that night.

The following morning was clean, bright and sunny and the steam hammer in my head had slowed to a gentler rhythm. And I felt hungry. Gerard was already up and whistling to himself as he fiddled about cooking breakfast.

'You sound better than you did yesterday,' I said, sniffing the air appreciatively. I was definitely improving.

'Aye,' answered Gerard, 'I'm on the mend. Thank God I had the sense to stay off the hard stuff. A thick head is bad enough but a pain in the guts is a real killer.'

'I suppose George hasn't surfaced yet?' I said.

'Oh, he will. It takes a lot to sink him for long.'

He was right and half an hour later George appeared, full of beans and demanding to know when he was going to get his breakfast. George had a wife back in Dublin so he was used to having little problems like that taken care of. We were back in the land of the living.

As the morning wore on the aches and pains of yesterday gradually disappeared and we decided to clear up the cottage, which was still littered with the debris of the party. Then we thought we'd take all the empties that had accumulated during our stay back to Roundstone. This was no easy task and the dinghy sat low in the water by the time it was loaded, leaving little room for passengers. Before we had even cleared the harbour George started to complain that he was cramped, so we gave him an ultimatum. He could shut up, row to Roundstone, or be put ashore. He kept quiet.

Gerard cocked his head up at the spectators looking over the sea wall in Roundstone, watching us unload the empties onto the quay. 'I'd give an eye tooth to know what's going on inside their skulls,' he said.

I was too busy to reply and wiped the sweat from my eyes as we hoisted the crates up out of the dinghy. It was hard work.

'Jesus, my arms feel like lumps of lead,' said George when the last one was ashore. He wiped an arm over his forehead and draped himself across a bollard.

'Hey, Jim, make sure you tie up the dinghy good and proper,' said Gerard.

'I need a drink, not a Boy Scout lecture,' I answered indignantly. I thought I must have lost a gallon of sweat lugging those crates ashore.

George was already marching for Connolly's. We were hardly in the door when Carmel lit on us.

'I heard all about ye,' she giggled. 'A naked woman doing a belly dance. Ye kept her out of sight.' Her eyes rolled in merriment.

Gerard's sunburnt face cracked in a wide grin. He winked. 'Smasher, she was. Mind you, the legs were a bit hairy.'

She guffawed and shook her head at us. 'Poor Mick, the auld fella was fit for nothing the next day, so I was told.'

George was the only one brave enough to order a Guinness. The very thought of it turned my stomach. In spite of his crack about young fellows not being able to hold their drink, I had a lemonade.

'We could hear you, you know. Clear as a bell in the town it was. A terrible racket,' Carmel continued. 'The party was a big success – they haven't stopped talking about it since.' She wiped the counter with a cloth and set our drinks before us. 'Poor Mick, he got a soaking an' he was asleep on his feet before they got him home. 'Tis a miracle he wasn't drowned or that he didn't catch his death of cold.'

George swallowed a sizeable gulp of Guinness and smacked his lips. 'Jesus, I was ready for that.'

'Listen to the man,' said Gerard. 'You'd think a drop hadn't passed his lips for months.'

Carmel prodded us relentlessly for information, firing streams of questions at us as we stuffed ourselves with sandwiches. Gerard and George rewarded her with a wildly funny account of the festivities. Some of it was news to me, presumably bits that I had missed when I was flat on my back. By the time we left to deal with mundane things such as groceries and the mail, she had enough stories to entertain her customers for months.

'We'll miss the three of ye when ye leave,' she called after us.

We looked at each other, smiling at our new-found celebrity status.

'I wouldn't try getting a jar of Guinness on the strength of it,' said Gerard.

There wasn't much time left in which to try. The holiday was coming to an end; George was leaving on Friday morning; the last few days went very quickly. Knowing that his time on the island was nearly over, George worked frantically at adding drawings and watercolours to the considerable pile he had already amassed. Some of the work he did in that final flurry was among the best he had done during his stay on Inishlacken. As I watched him leaf through them, I asked on the spur of the moment if he would let me have one. He signed and dated two watercolours and handed them to me.

'Here, have these to remind you of all the bloody laughs you've had at my expense,' he said.

'My God' – Gerard rolled his eyes – 'laughs? You're bloody kidding. Climbing the walls, pacifying you and putting up with your tantrums would be more like it.'

He was smiling as he said it and I knew that despite all their arguing and all their verbal punch-ups, they were genuinely the best of friends. I was glad to have spent so much time in their company.

We spent George's last evening in Connolly's. The locals, knowing he was leaving, congregated round our table to wish him well. Closing time came and went without any suggestion that we ought to leave. The doors were quietly bolted and the lights over the bar dimmed as we continued talking and drinking until, at last, we decided it was time to go and slipped outside into the cool night air. George's back got some more pounding before we were allowed to set off for the dinghy.

The good wishes of the fishermen cheered us on our way across the channel. In the starlight Inishlacken was only a hump on the horizon, its presence betrayed by the distant boom of the surf. As usual I was elected ferryman while the other two took their ease, content to let me navigate through the starry darkness. Up to now we had survived most of our night crossings with dry feet. Not this night. We had forgotten to check the state of the tide. It was three-quarters out and we had to wade through the slimy rocks, slipping and sliding in and out of shallow pools of water.

'God, my socks will be wringing wet,' complained George. 'I'll be sitting in the bus all the way home with wet boots.'

'And Madge will tan your arse for arriving in that state,' prophesied Gerard.

The two of them were sitting by the fire for their usual evening yarn and this time, since it was George's last one on the island, I sat up with them to enjoy the crack and the music from Gerard's gramophone.

The next day dawned warm and lovely, with dew-spangled spiders' webs and turf smoke spiralling upwards into a deep blue sky. George sat on the bench outside, watching the procession of sparkling waves rolling in from the

Atlantic. Lost in his thoughts, he did not hear me when I sat down beside him.

'Well, George, it's nearly time to go. Will you be glad to get back to Dublin?'

He looked at the vista before him and shook his head. 'On a day like this? With a view like that? I don't know whether I am or not.'

'Ach, you're a townie at heart, come on, admit it. Living out here the isolation would flip your lid sooner or later.'

He chewed this over, considering whether my assertion was one that needed to be hotly rejected or a compliment that could be cautiously accepted.

'Aye, in a way you might be right. This sort of thing is all right in small doses but I do miss the convenience of living in town. Christ, imagine running out of lead white halfway through a painting! You'd have to go to Galway to get even a new brush.' He strained against the back of the bench and stretched his legs. 'It's different for Gerard. He fits in here like a glove. I wouldn't have his patience or self-sufficiency to stay here for a year. Jesus, just imagine those long dark winter nights! And I don't have Gerard's close relationship with the countryside. I'm sure his paintings succeed because of the intimacy he has with the landscape and the people.'

George paused and then cocked his head as we heard the sound of old Séamus's stick clicking up the path. He rounded the corner, breaking into a broad grin as he spotted us. I could hear his bones creaking as he dropped awkwardly onto the bench beside us.

'Are ye leaving us, then?' he asked.

'Aye, Séamus. It's time to head back to Dublin. I've been here a month and if I stay any longer my wife will be suing for a divorce.'

'Don't listen to him, Séamus,' I said. 'It's our cooking. He can't stand it any longer. And the geese chased him halfway round the island again yesterday.'

Séamus slapped his knees with glee and Gerard came out to see what was going on.

'Séamus came over to say cheerio to George. He reckons he'll be dreaming of being chased by geese.'

'Will ye be back again?' Séamus asked.

George said that he wasn't sure.

'We'll be missing ye,' said the old man sincerely.

Two more figures suddenly appeared trudging steadily towards us.

'Here's Pádraig and Michael,' said Séamus. 'Yous nearly missed him,' he shouted as they got to the gate. 'He's ready to go.'

'Not without me, he isn't,' said Michael. 'I'm the one who's rowing him across in the currach.'

This was news to me but I was very happy to be rowed by someone else for a change. I could see that George was not so keen but he would have to grin and bear it. His last chance of a trip in a currach. Pádraig and Séamus shook

George long and hard by the hand, wished him well and tried to persuade him to return soon.

'I might just do that,' replied George. 'If not to Inishlacken then at least to Roundstone.'

At last we got George's luggage and ourselves aboard the currach and set off for Roundstone. Gerard and I offered to help with the rowing but Michael insisted on doing it himself. He threaded his way effortlessly through the harbour mouth and across the channel whilst engaging us in cheerful conversation. Only George looked glum as he sat in the stern surrounded by his possessions, no doubt contemplating the fact that there was only the thickness of tarred canvas between him and the abyss.

This time we approached Roundstone by the harbour rather than by the beach. We lugged George's suitcase and guitar to the bus stop opposite Connolly's to wait for the bus – invariably late. Gerard growled in exasperation but George decided to run over to the pub to say goodbye to Carmel.

'If the bus comes, give me a shout,' he said as he dashed across the road.

'Don't be drinking too much,' Gerard yelled after him, 'or you'll be holding your legs crossed before you get to Galway.'

A few minutes later the bus appeared over the brow of the hill. It freewheeled down and stopped with a squeal of brakes outside the bar. George didn't need to rush himself. The passengers disembarked, taking their time and without interrupting the flow of their conversations as they gathered their bits and pieces. Then the driver hopped down for a stretch and a smoke. Ten minutes had gone by before the engine spluttered into smoky life and George extricated himself from Connolly's to much back-thumping and a chorus of cheerios.

'Watch yourself in Dublin with all that traffic flying about,' said Gerard with a farewell grin.

'It'll be better than being chased by geese,' retorted George, grinning back at us.

Before he disappeared into the bus I reminded him that I would see him again in a fortnight's time on my way home to Belfast. We watched as he struggled along the aisle of the bus to the rear seat, and then the gearbox crunched and the bus lurched forward in a series of jolts as it got up speed. Our last glimpse of George was of him laughing from the rear window and waving frantically to us as the bus carried him away.

'Well, he's off, back to home cooking,' said Gerard. 'Madge will be delighted to be skivvying for him again.'

That evening it was remarkable how quiet the cottage was. I missed George. It was impossible not to. Even when he was sitting reading he was noisy, emitting little grunts and snorts of heavy breathing because of his catarrh. Reading rarely occupied him for long. Within a few minutes the book would be put down so that he could talk. Arguments were his life's blood and the more heated they were the more he enjoyed them. Gerard and I did not often

get the edge on him. I doubt if anyone did.

As we sat by the fire that evening I asked Gerard if he thought that George had enjoyed the last month. He kept me sucking on my pipe as he considered his answer. He turned a turf and we watched it explode in a shower of sparks.

'Some of the time I think he did, but country life cramps his restless style. He's a man for doing things on the spur of the moment. You know and I know that life in the sticks needs a bit of forward planning. That's not for George. I'll bet you he's in the pub at this minute with Madge and some of his cronies, telling them about the hardships he's had to endure and the struggle it was to survive. That's George.' He dropped another piece of turf on the fire and sat back in his chair.

'This morning, he said you fitted in here like a glove.'

Gerard looked sideways at me. 'That was an odd thing for him to say. What brought that on?'

'I asked him if he was looking forward to going home and one thing led to another. He said that your paintings are good because you feel at one with the landscape and the people.'

'The wee git! That's a turnabout – you heard him the other night.'

I remembered. It was during one of their more heated exchanges. So heated that at one point I thought they were going to end up punching one another. It had started with an innocent remark by George about a detail on one of Gerard's paintings and developed into a ferocious verbal battle in the course of which George told Gerard that he was narrow and provincial. There were a lot of things said then that I think they both regretted later. Usually their spats were good-natured and transient. They just liked to wind each other up for the hell of it. But if the subject of their paintings ever got into the fray, things could get very personal and one of them would take offence.

With George gone, my last fortnight on the island fell into a quiet pattern of eating, walking, talking, drawing and painting, punctuated by trips to Roundstone. Our waking and sleeping hours were much more regular now. The weather never changed. I woke half-expecting to see grey rain clouds sweeping in from the Atlantic but instead every morning dawned bright and blue. We were burnt nut-brown by the sun.

Each morning I would disappear to struggle with my drawings and watercolours, leaving Gerard at his easel. Both he and George were able to look at a landscape and reproduce it with all the unimportant elements eliminated, so that their work succeeded time after time. I did not yet have this

Old Séamus (left) and Gerard (right) with one of the islanders

ability and for the life of me I could not figure out how to acquire it. Compared with Gerard and George, I thought my work was far too detailed. They told me again and again that I was attempting too much on too broad a scale. Over the past four weeks I had seen the two of them produce, apparently without effort, beautiful pen and ink sketches, pencil drawings and watercolours. Often I had been green with envy. They had offered their advice freely: use bigger brushes, float the colours together, learn different combinations of colours to create a range of more subtle shades, and above all, concentrate on where the white paper should be left untouched. Watercolours demand a greater degree of intense concentration than oils. One mistake can ruin a watercolour irretrievably.

Gerard once gave me an intensive close-range lesson which saved me hours of unproductive painting and in my last days on Inishlacken I began to paint watercolours that I thought had some merit. I worked in a frenzy as my new-found expertise drove me to cover sheet after sheet with colour, and at last, looking over my shoulder one day, Gerard told me that banging my head against the proverbial brick wall had finally paid dividends.

With only a few more days to go I began to take stock of what I had done on the island. Underneath my bed I had stacked a pile of drawings and watercolours that I went through every so often, looking for those that I thought might make studies for oil paintings. On some I had pencilled colour notes in the margins. Months later, back in Belfast, I found myself wishing that I had done this more often. The notes were invaluable as a means of jogging my memory about a place or a subject that I had found

Ruins, Inishlacken
by Gerard Dillon

completely different from anything I was used to. Previously, I had painted mostly Belfast street scenes and I had found the straight vertical lines of the buildings a constraint on composition. Now I had discovered an exciting landscape without a straight line in sight. The Connemara countryside was like a roller coaster sweeping up and down in all directions. It had banished tall chimneys, iron gates and brick walls for a long time to come.

When it was time to leave I thought I might have at least two hundred sketches and watercolours, enough material to keep me painting for months. My earlier drawings of the island showed how inept I had been at capturing the strange and beautiful landscape just outside the cottage door. With hindsight I now realised that I had been overwhelmed, punch drunk even, by the multitude of shapes and patterns before me. I compared the first sketches with my latest work. There was no doubt that I had improved. The watercolours outlined broad shapes and colour masses into a mingling of earth, sky and sea. I was delighted to have my opinion confirmed by an approving Gerard.

'That's what it's all about,' he said.

During our time on the island George, Gerard and I had talked a great deal about art and our willingness to suffer deprivation in its cause. We had discussed the difficulty of finding somewhere to exhibit our work and the feeling of vulnerability that arose as a result of this insecurity.

'We are beggars, hanging our paintings on a wall and hoping that some damn fool will buy one and we will make enough to cover the cost of materials and

framing with a bit left over for breakfast,' Gerard had said.

'Well,' George had replied, 'we've chosen to do it, haven't we? Or has it chosen us?'

In any case, we knew we would carry on, unable to call a halt.

I had spent four and a half years training to be a motor mechanic and walked out six months before my apprenticeship ended to take up my career as an artist. All three of us had been in secure employment and thrown it all up, driven by a lunatic compulsion to paint. None of us had been to art school. We were all self-taught. I was only seventeen when I first met George. I owed him a lot: he had fanned the urge to express myself in paint and in the past few weeks I felt that both George and Gerard had helped me a great deal.

Soon it was the evening of my last day on Inishlacken. I took a final long walk along the humpy paths, past slumbering cottages scenting the air with the smell of burning turf. Along the rocky foreshore, the sky was streaked with crimson and orange and a blood-red sun dipped below the horizon, leaving long purple shadows. The geese, thank heaven, were shut in for the night as I dandered leisurely up to say my farewells to Pádraig and Michael.

Michael offered to row me to Roundstone in the morning but I wanted to have one last row to end the holiday. It would be a long time before I got the opportunity to row a dinghy again. Old Séamus gave me a dunt on the shoulder and told me to be sure to come back. I smiled, shook hands, and wished him good luck. I stood on a little peninsula, looking out at the vast rim

James and his
future wife, 1951

of the Atlantic, and felt a sadness at leaving. What a marvellous holiday it had
been! I was going home, fit as a fiddle, mentally stimulated, ready to attack my
painting with renewed energy.

I had another reason for returning to Belfast. I had met a beautiful young
woman with eyes as black as coal pots and cheeks like golden honey. The
thought of her made my toes curl. I couldn't wait to see her again.

Next morning in Roundstone I climbed aboard a post office van that would
take me to Galway to catch the train to Dublin. Inside was another passenger,
an Australian girl who was on a hiking tour of Ireland. Gerard stood in the
bright sunshine, grinning. He gave me a final wave as the metal doors clanged
shut behind me. The road to Galway town was long and bumpy and I was on
my way home.

James's Inishlacken exhibition,
55A Donegall Place, Belfast,
1952

EPILOGUE

I wasn't to return to Inishlacken until forty years later. This time I was alone. Gerard had died of a stroke in 1971 and George of a brain haemorrhage in 1979. In 1991 I went to Inishlacken to take part in a television programme about Gerard's life and career. His paintings now fetch thousands of pounds, a far cry from that shared summer when we had to make every halfpenny count.

Sitting with the television crew in the stern of the fishing boat chugging across the channel, I recalled that summer of 1951. Did I really row a dinghy with two inebriated passengers all the way from Roundstone to Inishlacken? It seemed a long way. My hair stood on end as I remembered the nights I had rowed in pitch darkness, oblivious of the maritime hazards.

We anchored off the island. A dinghy took us through the harbour, looking narrower than when I had shot through it with my passengers many years earlier. The tide was out. Once again I had to scramble over seaweed-shrouded rocks and wade through pools. I was not so agile now. It had changed. Forty years ago the little harbour had been crammed with upturned currachs resting on the green verges surrounding the sandy beach. Now there was not one to be seen.

The beach was deserted. I looked beyond. There was our cottage gleaming white in the midday sun but the original blue doors and window frames were stained a dull oak-brown. The wild flower garden had been swamped by overgrown grass. Our open door was now shut and a huge lock replaced the old black latch. Curtains were tightly drawn across the windows to keep out

inquisitive eyes. But our bench was still there. I sat on it, looking out to sea, while the cameramen set up their equipment.

Memories flooded back of acrimonious debates as we lay in the sun, arguing the toss about this and that. The cameras followed me as I walked along the stone paths, now a solid mass of grass growing unhindered by the tread of passing feet. A sad, deserted air hung over the island, without even the bleat of a sheep to disturb the silence. The last of the islanders had left for the mainland in 1975; now most of the cottage roofs had caved in, leaving gaping window frames rotting in the stone walls. I looked in vain for our well on the beach but winter winds and fierce gales had piled sand and boulders over that corner by the cottage. I guessed the well was drowned under sand for ever. Who would think of looking for a freshwater well on a beach washed by the Atlantic?

Two or three cottages were still in good shape because they were used as holiday houses. The week before our visit the local paper had carried an advertisement for the sale of the old schoolhouse with its private beach.

The island I knew had vanished like a dream. Never again would the mornings ring with the laughter of children waiting for the school currach. Never again would Michael, Pádraig or old Séamus come along the path for a jar and a bit of crack while watching the waves surge in and out of the harbour.

I wandered back toward the waiting sea, picking my way around the rocks scattered across the beach and smiling as I remembered George leapfrogging them, cursing loud enough to raise the devil as he desperately struggled to shake off the crab locked onto his fingers. As I sat on the harbour watching the ebb tide froth through the boulders, I recalled the nights when we splashed and blasphemed our way through them, hauling our dinghy behind us. I will never know why we didn't break a leg.

The cottage, slumbering in the golden light of the afternoon sun, focused my mind on the memory of Gerard and George sprawled on the bench, their heads wagging over the inevitable argument, their laughter drifting over the harbour. I smiled to myself, thinking about how much fun we had got out of George's antics and misfortunes. It was unbearably sad that I had had to return by myself. What crack we would have had if there had been the three of us here.

The silence hugged itself close, wrapping memories of that summer around me. Images floated through my mind to be replaced time and time again as I remembered those days and nights of so long ago.

Laughter and approaching footsteps abruptly shattered my daydreams. The film crew had returned to stack their equipment on the quayside to await the ferry we could see returning to the island.

'Thank God, it's all safely in the can. We were very lucky with the weather today,' said the producer.

We had been delayed in Roundstone for two days to let the weather settle down enough for us to go across and land on Inishlacken.

'Not a bit like the last time I was here,' I told him.

Halfway down the harbour steps I stopped to give our cottage and the past a final salute. No, it was not a bit like last time.

ACKNOWLEDGEMENTS

I could not have written this book without the generous assistance of my friends and I would like to thank: Bill Stanley, who goaded, persuaded and offered his talents unstintingly; Anne Calvert, for reading the manuscript and giving invaluable advice; Pauline McLarnon, for typing my rewrites; Gerard Dillon who, from somewhere, unearthed his uncle's Inishlacken photographs; Esler Crawford and Paul Parkhill, who solved my photographic problems; and Moore Sinnerton, reviver of Inishlacken memories.

And finally Mike, my wife, who suffered a winter's-long silence as I scribbled in the corner and, ultimately, argued the not so finer points of my English when she typed the final manuscript. As usual, she won most of the arguments.

PUBLISHERS' ACKNOWLEDGEMENTS

Grateful acknowledgement is made to the copyright holders for permission to reproduce the following illustrations:

page ii, *Milking Time, Roundstone* by James MacIntyre (from a private collection); page 15, *The Harbour, Roundstone* by James MacIntyre (from a private collection); page 16, photograph (courtesy of Gerard Dillon); page 18, *The Yellow Bungalow* by Gerard Dillon (courtesy of the Trustees of the Ulster Museum, Belfast); page 21, photograph (courtesy of Gerard Dillon); page 27, *Island People* by Gerard Dillon (courtesy of the Crawford Municipal Art Gallery, Cork); page 30, *House, Main Street, Roundstone* by James MacIntyre (from a private collection); page 31, *Kate O'Brien's House, Roundstone* by James MacIntyre (from a private collection); page 39, photograph (courtesy of Gerard Dillon); page 53, *Inishlacken* by George Campbell (from a private collection); page 60, *Connemara Landscape* by George Campbell (from a private collection); page 65, *Man with Lamp* by Gerard Dillon (from a private collection); page 87, *Pub Scene* by George Campbell (from a private collection); page 89, *The Lobster Pots* by Gerard Dillon (from a private collection); page 123, photograph (courtesy of Gerard Dillon); page 136, *Turf Carrier, Roundstone* by James MacIntyre (from a private collection); page 139, photograph (courtesy of Gerard Dillon); page 140, *Ruins, Inishlacken* by Gerard Dillon (from a private collection); page 144, *Main Street, Roundstone* by James MacIntyre (from a private collection); page 146, photograph (courtesy of Gerard Dillon); page 147, photograph (courtesy of Gerard Dillon); page 148, photograph (courtesy of Moore Sinnerton); page 149, photograph (courtesy of Moore Sinnerton).

All other illustrations in this book are owned by James MacIntyre.